The Lockerbie Disaster

30 years of Deceit (1988-2018)

By Robert John Simons

Perjury Press 2018

copyright 2018   © Robert John Simons

perjurypress@gmail.com

robertjohnsimons1638@gmail.com

Photo-spread shown to Tony Gauci 15th Feb. 1991

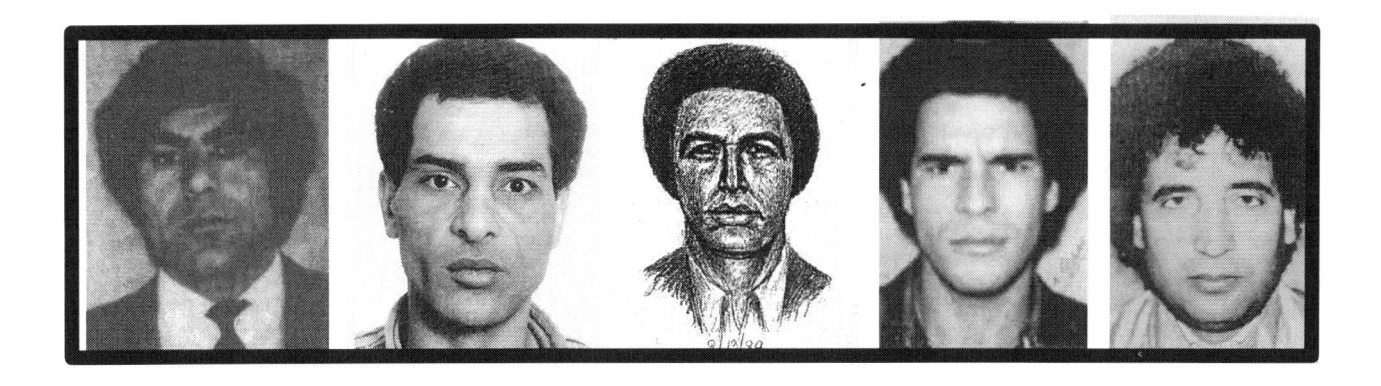

these images have 2 things in common

1] Tony Gauci claimed they all closely resembled the clothes buyer.
2] they look nothing like each other.

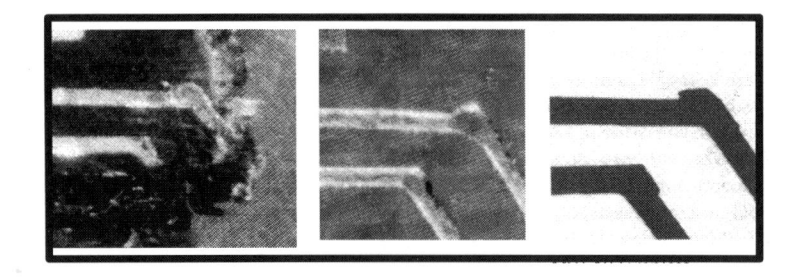

The above 3 images show the copper trackings of
the bomb fragment PT/35[b]
the sample circuit board made for MEBO
& the original template.
Note the identical design including imperfections. However the fragment from the bomb is a clever
imitation of the timers sold only to Libya.

Evidence label PI/995 hthe label has been carefully altered from "CLOTH" to "DEBRIS"

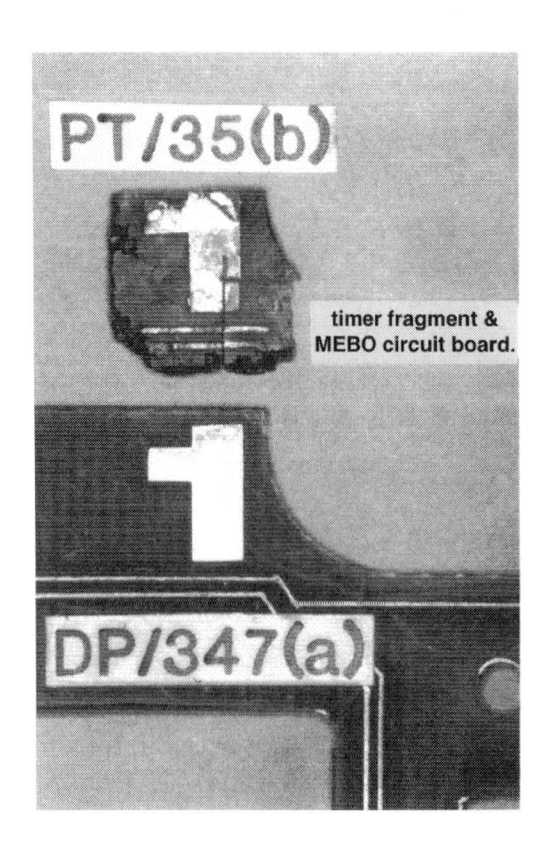

bomb fragment PT/35[b] & original MST-13 timer circuit board.

Dedication

To Dr. Jim Swire, whose simple love for a daughter, has sustained him for 30 years in his campaign for answers, justice, and accountability from those who should have warned the 259 people who thought it was safe to fly with Pan Am that fateful night. He is to me as 'Scottish' a hero as any born in our beautiful land.

And to the people of Lockerbie who with courage and dignity have refused to be defined by the events of Dec. 21st 1988.

special thanks to

Holly, Ellie, Aaron, James, James & Eileen.

contents.

introduction.

list of abbreviations.

the people involved.

overview of the Lockerbie bombing.

prologue.

the A-Z of Tony Gauci's confusing statements.

how to get rich and frame people.

the SCCRC uncovers the truth.

did Gauci really say he saw Megrahi?

paying witnesses is wrong.

the A-Z of the facts of the case.

a piece of fibreglass the size of a fingernail changes everything.

bad forensics convicted Megrahi, good forensics will clear him.

if in doubt blame Gadaffi.

suspicious evidence.

the A-Z of PT/35[b].

Thatcher benefits from not investigating Heathrow Airport.

conclusion.

further study.

introduction

The case against Abdelbaset Al Megrahi was very weak to begin with, after 2 main witnesses were exposed as liars, what remained were just inferences from poor forensics, a partial identification, and coincidence. Nothing more.

The official UN observer Hans Kochler was scathing in his report of the trial. Giving details of political interference he concludes:

"On the basis of the above observations and evaluation, the undersigned has - to his great dismay - reached the conclusion that the trial, seen in its entirety, was not fair and was not conducted in an objective manner. Indeed, there are many more questions and doubts at the end of the trial than there were at its beginning."

He also criticized the appeal:

"Regrettably, the decision of the Appeal Court in the case of Abdelbaset Ali Mohamed Al Megrahi v. H.M. Advocate was not a victory for justice, but for power politics."

Perhaps Scotland's leading legal authority, Professor Robert Black QC, was equally appalled by the verdict:

"The most disgraceful miscarriage of justice in Scotland for 100 years."

Since the verdict, what little evidence the Crown had has been totally discredited. Anyone following the facts of the case knows this. Should the SCCRC grant another appeal[1] it is a certainty that Megrahi will be cleared of all guilt for the Lockerbie bombing. What's needed now are not more facts. What we need is to apply pressure.

There are 5.3 *Million*[2] reasons for fighting Megrahi's conviction. That's how many people live in Scotland and we should *all* fear the judicial system as it stands.

Witnesses paid millions, evidence tampered with and possibly planted, police lying, crucial documents withheld from the defence, the Lord Advocate misleading the court, political pressure from a foreign government, forensic details hidden. All this happened in full view of the world's media.

If it can happen to Megrahi it can happen to *any of us*. Those in charge of the judicial process, will do all they can to prevent the embarrassment that would result from overturning the verdict against "the Lockerbie bomber."

But the reputations of our senior judges, or the police, or the Lord Advocate are nothing compared to fair and transparent JUSTICE. Whatever the shame that will follow, we have no choice. The reputation of Scotland's once great judicial system is in *tatters*. The UN observer, MEPs, church leaders, & many other groups have called for a UN led independent inquiry, into what they see as a travesty of justice. We need to swallow our pride as a nation and restore confidence in our legal system. I urge you to join the '*Justice for Megrahi*' campaign, for the sake of you, your children, your neighbors.

And pray they are not accused of a crime until the problem of our justice system is fixed.

---

[1] They previously found 6 grounds where Megrahi may have suffered a miscarriage of justice, and since then new information has come to light that proves he was not involved.
[2] 2015 population estimate.

list of abbreviations.

AAIB Air Accident Investigation Branch.
AVE4041 The plane's luggage container which contained the bomb.
BATF Bureau of Alcohol, Tobacco and Firearms, a US Federal Agency.
BKA West Germany's Police.
CIA The Central Intelligence Agency.
Camp Zeist. Neutral venue for the trial (in Holland but under Scottish legal jurisdiction).
DIA Defense Intelligence Agency, a US Federal agency.
D&G Dumfries & Galloway Police, who led the investigation.
FBI Federal Bureau of Investigation a US Federal Agency.
GCHQ monitors all electronic communications, telephones, and other conversations etc. for UK government.
IRA Irish Republican Army.
JSO Libya's equivalent of MI5.
LAA Libyan Arab Airlines.
MI5 British Security Service.
MI6 British Secret Intelligence Service.
MEBO AG Swiss company who supplied MST timers to Libyan Military.
MOD Ministry of Defence.
Mossad Israeli Intelligence Service.
MST-13 a timer device alleged to be from the bomb. Only 20 MST's were made: all for the Libyan Military.
NSA National Security Agency. Monitors foreign communications that may threaten the USA.
NUM National Union of Mine workers.
PA103 or PanAm103 The plane which blew up over Lockerbie.
PCB Printed Circuit Board.
PFLP-GC Popular Front for Liberation of Palestine General Command. A violent rival of the PLO. Works with Palestine Popular Struggle Front PPSF.
PPSF Palestine Popular Struggle Front. Another PLO rival.
PLO Palestine Liberation Organization. The major group fighting Israel's occupation.
PT/35[b] a tiny piece of circuit board allegedly from the bomb. The most important fragment of forensic evidence in the case.
RARDE Royal Armaments Research & Development Establishment. The Forensics specialists who examine evidence in terrorist attacks.
RTZ Rio Tinto Zinc a major mining corporation.
SCCRC Scottish Criminal Cases Review Commission. An independent body that decides if miscarriages of justice have occurred. Their 800 page Report said this likely happened to Megrahi.
STASI East German secret service.
Thuring AG. Swiss electronic manufacturers who made the printed circuit boards, or PCBs for MEBO.
UN The United Nations.

the major people in the Lockerbie case.

the good guys:

Abdelbaset al **Megrahi**. Only suspect found guilty of the Lockerbie bombing. Died of cancer 2012.

Lamin **Fhimah**, associate and co accused of the bombing. Acquitted of all charges.

The **SCCRC** who recommended a fresh appeal, their clinical analysis was in stark contrast to the 3 judges who found Megrahi guilty.

Dr. Jim **Swire**, father of victim Flora, more than anyone he has campaigned courageously and never wavered in his demand for justice and accountability.

Robert **Black** QC, architect of the trial in a neutral country (his biggest regret), and campaigner for Megrahi's innocence, his desire is to restore Scottish justice's integrity.

Morag **Kerr**, forensics genius who proved the bomb was planted at Heathrow.

John **Ashton**, investigator & researcher for Megrahi's 2nd appeal, author of *Megrahi:You Are My Jury*.

David **Wolchover**, Barrister, author of *Culprits of Lockerbie*. He examines every single thread of evidence & point by point demolishes the case against Megrahi.

the bad guys:

Ahmed **Jibril**, leader of the PFLP-GC, responsible for many airplane bombings.

Abu **Elias**, likely Jibril's nephew and possible suspect in placing the bomb.

Marwan **Khreesat**, bomb maker for the PFLP-GC and Jordanian double agent.

Hafez **Dalkamoni**, head of the German cell of the terror group.

Mohamed Abu **Talb**, terrorist convicted of many bombings in Europe, may have bought the clothes in the suitcase.

the liars:

Edwin **Bollier**, co-owner of swiss electronics company MEBO, and a major crown witness in trial.

Abdul Majid **Giaka**, colleague of Megrahi and Fhimah at Libyan Airlines, turned CIA super-grass and "star witness."

Tony & Paul **Gauci** co owners of Mary's House boutique in Malta, where the clothes in the bomb case were bought. Paid over $3Million dollars as "witnesses."

The **Crown Prosecution**, who deceived the Court, withheld witnesses, documents, and forensics.

the scientists:

Dr Thomas **Hayes**, forensic expert at RARDE.

Mr Allen **Feraday**, lead forensic examiner at RARDE.

Tom **Thurman**, FBI forensic examiner.

others:

Margaret **Thatcher**, Britain's Prime Minister 1979-1990.

Arthur **Scargill**, leader of the miners during the 1984-85 strike.

Lord **Carrington**, Foreign Secretary for Mrs Thatcher.

Colonel **Gadaffi**, Libyan Dictator.

overview of the Lockerbie bombing.

Dec 21st 1988, Pan Am 103 explodes over Lockerbie Killing 270 innocent people. At first a cell of Palestinian terrorists in Germany is suspected, acting for Iran in revenge for a plane shot down by the USA 6 months before Lockerbie.

The police investigate Frankfurt airport. One record suggests the bomb might have come from Malta in an unaccompanied suitcase.

Clothes in the suitcase came from a shop in Malta, The shopkeeper describes a Libyan man as the buyer.

A fragment of a timer from the bomb is discovered. This timer points to Libya.

In 1991, the 2 Libyans are indicted for the bombing. 9 years later they are tried.

One goes free & one goes to jail. Most people including legal experts don't buy it.

In 2007 the SCCRC reports a possible miscarriage of justice. Megrahi is granted a new appeal but finds he is terminally ill with cancer.

He is released on compassionate grounds having first given up his appeal.

In 2012 he dies in Tripoli at home but still known as "the Lockerbie bomber".

More evidence emerges that would destroy the verdict. The main witness was paid $2million. The timer fragment is a very careful imitation of the Libyan ones.[3]

2014 Operation Sandwood investigates police malpractice, tampering with evidence, perjury.
2016 it will soon report its findings.
2018 it will soon report its findings.

May 2018 the SCCRC considers another appeal, requested by Megrahi's family.

Dec 2018, 30 years on and we still don't know what happened.

Almost every piece of evidence against Megrahi is now discredited. The Scottish government still refuses to hold an inquiry.

---

[3] Inevitably cries of "conspiracy theory" will be leveled at the idea of fabricated evidence. Ok, Lockerbie has spawned a wild conspiracy theory or ten. But real conspiracies do exist. The bomb that caused Lockerbie got on the plane as the result of a concerted *conspiracy* by the terrorists. The issue is whether there is cogent, consistent evidence to confirm a conspiracy or just conjecture that has no basis in fact.

prologue.

LOCKERBIE, Scotland 21ˢᵗ December 1988, 7:05pm

The scene is like something from Dante's inferno. It is the winter solstice, the longest night of the year. The blackness of night broken by the orange flames and searing heat.

I am **Flora MacDonald Swire** I was just 23 years old. By the time my flight was to land in New York I would have been 24. Just 2 minutes ago I was relaxing on Pan Am flight 103 to New York, looking forward to spending Christmas with my boyfriend, 31,000 feet above Scotland in a Boeing 747 Jumbo jet (unbeknown to all of us there had been very specific warnings of a bomb: a violent Palestinian terror group was targeting a Pan Am flight from Europe to the USA. Security ought to have been extra vigilant, but was not). Then the explosion. The plane torn apart. 270 of us murdered.

Now it's like a scene from Hell: acrid smoke, wreckage, twisted metal, ruined houses and corpses strewn around. On the ground, on roofs, hanging from trees.

The smell is awful but it's not sulphur I smell. It is jet fuel and burning flesh. There are 20 bodies in one garden alone, another 60 embedded all over the fairways of the nearby golf course.

Groups of numb, speechless souls stand around the burning houses unable to take in the horror of what has just happened. 259 of us fell from the jet black night sky, some still strapped into their seats. Our lives ended in a split-second by a terrorist's bomb in a brown Samsonite suitcase. Another 11 tragic residents of Sherwood Crescent, Lockerbie, a friendly, sleepy little Scots town near the border with England. Killed when the Boeing's fuselage carved out a massive crater where their homes had been this morning. The fuel filled wings ignite sending a fireball 300ft into the air.

Motive?

Less than 6 months ago, 171 days in fact, the same tragic end befell 290 innocents of Iranian Airbus flight 655. Shot down in Iranian airspace by the gung-ho Captain Wm. Rogers of the USS *Vincennes*. He mistook a giant passenger jet for an F-14 fighter jet. Rogers lied to cover his crime. He said the plane was descending rapidly towards them ready to attack: actually it was climbing, slowly within the known *civilian* flight corridor. He said it changed course towards them: in fact it stayed on course and was 20 miles away when he shot it down.

He alleged Iranian gun-boats had attacked them earlier: in fact it was the *Vincennes* that had entered Iran's territorial waters to provoke a response[4].

---

[4] The US was patrolling the gulf, to protect oil tankers from Iraq and Kuwait to make sure their oil got to market. While they were often attacking Iranian ships they never ever attacked Iraqi boats. Even when Saddam

Other warships in the area watched in horror as Rogers (Robo-Cruiser was their nickname for him) ordered the plane to be shot down. At best it was criminal negligence and at worst a deliberate war crime.

Instead of a tribunal President George Bush Snr. gave Rogers and the whole crew medals. He even boasted *"he would never apologize for America- no matter the facts,"* and refused liability or compensation. [Douglas Boyd describes Iran's "Qisas" or revenge similar to an eye for an eye. Had the US accepted its mistake, made compensation it is likely Iran would have called off any attack].

Iran swore revenge. The Ayatollah denounced the crime and the prime minister ordered a rumoured $10 Million be paid to the Syrian based terrorist Ahmed Jibril and his PFLP-GC to blow up an American passenger jet to avenge all those bloated bodies filmed floating in the Gulf, 66 of them children.

I blame you Margaret Thatcher. You briefly expressed outrage for the Lockerbie bombing and empathy for the victims. Sadly your response to Iran's innocents was to jump to America's defence. While the whole world condemned US actions you blamed Iran, backed the lie that it provoked the earlier attack, blamed the victims for descending towards the USS Vincennes (they hadn't) and told Iran to end the war with Iraq that you had done all you could to prolong by arming both sides, but especially Saddam Hussein.

Had you not blindly defended the indefensible maybe Britain would not have suffered its worst ever terror attack.

Margaret Thatcher You don't know that.

Flora How did British intelligence respond to the bomb threat? It seems they didn't. The US warned its diplomats of a very specific bomb threat targeting Pan Am flights. South African foreign minister Pik Botha and his entourage are rumoured to have cancelled their seat reservations that morning and taken a different plane. But your security experts dismissed the threats as a hoax and crucially chose not to warn the British public of the threat. Why was Heathrow not put on high alert? Extra security, extra vigilance might have saved us.

Even worse was your treatment of the victims' families who just wanted to know the truth. Your Transport Secretary Cecil Parkinson told the families he would get a full public enquiry into the disaster but you blocked it.[5] This was unprecedented for the worst terrorist attack ever in the UK. What was there to hide?

Hussein attacked the USS Stark killing 37 American servicemen, Reagan dismissed it as an accident, and even blamed Iran.

[5] Both the King's Cross rail disaster (31 died) and Piper Alpha disaster (167 died) merited public enquiries and yet Lockerbie killed more than those two tragedies combined.

Worse still you refused to even *meet* with a delegation of the victims' families and this was just the start of your failure to do the decent thing. As a rule if you *could* make a situation worse you *did*.

Ordinary victims make for good PR- they make you seem human. But politics, personal connections, or greed always triumphed over justice where you were concerned. When President Bush asked you to play down the investigation of Iran[6] and Syria it appears you were happy to acquiesce. D&G Police Supt. Pat Connor wrote a report on the PFLP-GC, he wanted to issue arrest warrants for 15 (Palestinian) suspects. Paul Channon, your then Transport Secretary, briefed journalists that arrests were imminent. He was branded a liar when you denied it was true. For many reasons the investigation soon focussed on Libya. This book will look at the motives you might have had for shifting the blame onto Gadaffi and Libya.

You wrote 2 large volumes of memoirs but couldn't find time to mention Lockerbie- the biggest terrorist attack in UK history. Your heartless response was "I didn't know anything about Lockerbie and I never write about things I do not know about." That's your excuse? As PM you *should* have taken an interest and you should have made sure the police left no stone unturned. Made sure the forensics facility was fit for purpose and had a whole team of top scientists. Understaffed and with dozens of other cases, they took 3 years to process the evidence and complete their joint Report.

If this had been an IRA attack you would certainly have been interested. They were the only terrorists you ever cared about. Apart from the many you supported of course.[7] Or maybe if it had been a further 20 miles or so to the south, rather than in Scotland?

The above fictitious account imagines Flora Swire (from her place of rest) confronting Margaret Thatcher (from her place of torment) and asking her why the Lockerbie disaster happened. No disrespect to Flora's memory whatsoever is intended. She was a remarkable young woman.

---

[6] Most likely to aid the release of hostages in Lebanon.
[7] Like Osama Bin Laden and Gulbuddin Hekmatyar in Afghanistan; Pol Pot's Khmer Rouge in Cambodia; the Contras in Nicaragua to name just a few.

the A-Z of Tony Gauci's confusing statements.

Some of the clothes from the bomb suitcase were traced to a small family owned boutique, Mary's House in Malta, run by brothers Tony and Paul Gauci. Al Megrahi was alleged to have bought the clothes on the 7th Dec. 1988: just 2 weeks before the bombing. Below is a sample of Gauci's evidence. Issues like Christmas lights being on, whether it was raining, etc. were used to decide if the purchase was on the 7th Dec. or 23rd Nov. Megrahi was in Malta on 7/12/88 but not 23/11/88. Gauci often gave 2 or 3 versions of what he remembered.

He made as many as 23 police statements about the man who bought clothes in his shop. *He contradicted himself on nearly every little detail-* in his police statements, defence and Crown precognitions, and court testimony. Many of his contradictions were hidden from the defence. Thanks to the Scottish Criminal Cases Review Commission (SCCRC) we can see just how muddled Tony Gauci was. Curiously his testimony got closer to the Crown's case the more he read about it in magazines. You decide if he sounds credible or not.

He was asked about the identity of the man, what he bought, when he bought it, who was there, and so on, beginning with his first witness statement 9 MONTHS after Lockerbie. It would be Feb. of 1991, 2 years after the bombing, until Gauci finally picked Megrahi out from photo spreads. Everything is based on Gauci's own words taken from the written police statements, court precognitions,[8] court testimony, or interviews with the SCCRC.

a) He looked like him (Abu Talb). He looked like him (Al Megrahi). He was like this man (Mohamed Saleem). Or a lot of others too. (Gauci actually thought that Talb and Megrahi were the SAME guy!).

b) He was 6 feet or more tall. He was 6 feet or less. I never said over 6 feet. (Megrahi was only 5'8).

c) He was 50 or more years old. He was under 60. He was in his forties. (Megrahi was only 36 at the time).

d) He was dark skinned and well built. (Megrahi is light skinned and not well built). He had a large chest but not large waist. He is *not* the dark [skinned] one.

e) He bought no shirts. I never sold him any shirts for sure. That man bought no shirts! (then the police buy 2 shirts as samples) Now I remember he bought 2 shirts. It was blue.[9] It was green. It was beige.[10] It was blue and white striped. (had they kept asking he might have

---

[8] The process whereby prosecution and defence lawyers interview witnesses before trial.
[9] That's the shirt he "for sure" never sold!
[10] The Scottish police statement has scored out the word 'beige' as has the official HOLMES computer statement. Fortunately the Maltese officer DI Scicluna also took a statement with the word 'beige' intact.

eventually guessed the correct colour, which was actually grey)

f) They were size 16 ½ or 17 collar. (The shirt found was a 14 ½ collar so could not be the one Tony "remembered").

g) The exact amount of the sale was £76.50[11] I gave him £4.00 change. It was £56.00. I never said it was £56. No it was £77.00 I gave him £3.00 change. or £88.00, or £98.50[12] or ...

h) It was November or December. It was in the Winter. It was the 29th of November I remember because the same day my girlfriend broke up with me. He came in both November AND December! It was about 2 weeks before Christmas.

i) It was Midweek. I can't remember. It was not a Saturday.

j) It was raining. It was just a few drops. The ground was damp.

k) He (the man) went UP the street to get a taxi and I think I saw him get in a taxi. He went DOWN the street and 15 minutes later he returned in a taxi. I never saw him get in the taxi.

l) The taxi pulled up outside and the man got out. The taxi went round the corner and the man came back in the shop.

m) The man took the parcels (of clothes) and I saw him put them in the back seat of the taxi. I carried the parcels and *I* put them in the back seat of the Taxi. I asked Paul to watch the shop as I took the parcels to the taxi. *Paul* took the parcels to the taxi ACROSS THE STREET!

n) (when shown photo of Megrahi on many occasions Gauci said) – It is not him. It was a bit like him. It resembles a little. It "was him" (Maltese:"Tan Du"). It may have been him. I am 100% sure it was him. Not exactly the man but a little bit exactly the man I saw in the shop.

o) There were no Christmas lights outside. There were Christmas lights outside. They were just putting the Christmas lights up.

p) I never asked for money. I asked for money but only after the trial. (Police had to "shut him down *every time* he asked for reward money"[13] and "his brother Paul would do anything to get money" "[Paul] is always exaggerating his own importance as a witness," "[Paul]...has a clear desire to gain financial benefit," "the Gauci's had financial problems").[14]

---

[11] He was certain because the man paid with 8 x £10 notes and he gave him £4.00 change. This EXACT figure changed every time he "remembered" something else the man purchased.
[12] These last 2 are calculated by the SCCRC once the other "remembered" items are included.
[13] Crucially the interest in the reward money was almost certainly the day he picked Megrahi's photo. The payments (£3million) and Tony and Paul's demands were concealed from the defence and the court.
[14] Impact Assessment Report (12/1/01) [SCCRC Appendix: Protectively Marked Materials/D&G] - attached to letter of 7/2/01, which in support of a reward states:
(a) "the issue of financial remuneration has not been discussed *in detail* with the witnesses and no promises exist" (b) "It is considered that the witnesses may harbour some expectation of their situation being recognised, however whilst proceedings are still 'live' they displayed a clear understanding that such matters could not be

q) I was in the shop alone as Paul was watching a football match. Paul never came to the shop. Paul came back just as the man went to get a taxi. Paul came back as the man was leaving. Paul left just as the man arrived back. The man bought an umbrella because it was raining. I suggested to the man and he bought the umbrella.

r) He only came into my shop once. I never saw him before. He was in my shop a year or more before. I saw him in a pub. I took parcels to his hotel.

(On 26th Sept. 1989 Gauci went to police to say the same man came back yesterday).

s) This man was him. Or his identical twin. I am only 50% sure it was him.[15] It looked like him.

t) It was yesterday the 25th Sept. It was between the 21st and 24th September. (if his memory was so vague after *ONE* day how could he be trusted to remember someone 9 months before).

u) It was the day I argued with my girlfriend the 29th November, I remember because 'I split from her'. It was not just one occasion I fought with my girlfriend, we had lots of arguments. No I don't remember her name.

v) I do not recall having a girlfriend in 1988. I am always with someone.

w) She would cause arguments by suggesting a wedding day or that we buy expensive furniture. (Police statement "Mr Gauci had a girlfriend HE wished to marry but SHE did not want to marry him").

x) Maybe I am confused and was referring to Paul's girlfriend!

y) He bought a Babygro with a sheep's head motif on the front from "Big Ben" clothing. (when told that Big Ben didn't make such an item he said:) I'm not sure it had a sheep's head motif. (shown one with a lamb's body he says) I remember now it had a lambs body on front I am sure.

z) He bought a red and black checked cardigan I got from another shop. He bought TWO cardigans: A brown one and a blue one I got from an ex policeman. I didn't get it from a

---

explored" (c) "The conduct of the Gauci brothers reflects both their own integrity and their response to the manner with which the police have dealt with them. It is therefore vital that they continue to *perceive that their position is recognised* and they continue to receive the respect that their conduct has earned."
In other words they need to know they will get the reward money but that we can't discuss it until *after* the trial is over to maintain their "integrity." DC Bell swore that he had never mentioned reward money, however the SCCRC discovered his diaries and a memo which proved this was a pack of lies. As soon as the appeal was over Dumfries & Galloway Police wrote the US Dept of Justice to recommend they receive the reward money. Noting that a statute has just been passed to increase the award. Was $3million not enough? In light of this scandal we are entitled to know if *all* the money went to just the Gauci's.

[15] This change of mind was after just *one* month.

policeman. I bought it from Eagle Knitwear. He also bought 2 pullovers! (the cardigan was beige).

aa) I did see a photo in the papers of the accused. I was shown a picture by my brother. My neighbour would come in every day with pictures of the accused. My brother kept every article in a scrap book. I saw the article (with Megrahi's photo and the word "bomber") a short time. I had it at least 4 months.

bb) I saw the photos in It Torca[16] magazine. I didn't see the photos in It Torca magazine.

cc) He bought a Harris Tweed Jacket. The jacket was Italian style not like Tweed.

With a witness like this his evidence *was worse than useless*. How could the judges come to any conclusion based on a completely contradictory account of everything? How could the defence lawyers possibly know which tactics to choose? Or which evidence to introduce? If they had no idea which version of Gauci's statements he would suddenly "remember" or worse which version the judges were going to believe? This is why the whole trial was a farce in every important part and every *un*important part as well.

Had the police said the sale was in April, Gauci would have identified the Easter Bunny.

The 3 judges found Mr Gauci to be a "careful and credible witness"! Except for the fact that he was vague and confused. And contrary to all scientific studies of the mind his memory grew CLEARER the further away from the original events. So that at trial his memory was better than it had been 12 years ago.

---

[16] "*The Torch*" a local paper in Maltese language. These articles explained the details of the case and **most importantly**, where Tony's evidence contradicted their case. This may explain why in court he reversed his statements about the man's age, height, and the Christmas lights.

how to get rich and frame people.

Although 3 senior Scottish judges couldn't see a problem with the witnesses I would bet at *least a majority* of a jury of 15 ordinary Scots would have known exactly what to do: acquit the accused because the 3 chief witnesses were:

a) **Majid Giaka**: a proven liar[17] that the judges dismissed as totally untrustworthy, paid by the CIA and desperate to get $4 million reward money.

b) **Edwin Bollier**: a chancer that the judges found untruthful and motivated to get $4 Million reward money[18].

c) **Tony Gauci**: a totally confused old guy motivated to get and actually paid $2 Million reward money. His bro was given $1 Million[19] as well: a reward for keeping his "brother motivated to testify", and to "avoid any future problems" (i.e. the police thought he would be jealous of his brothers money and might spill the beans).

Abdul Majid Giaka defected to the CIA in September 1988, he was asked about Lockerbie and the role of Megrahi and Fhimah but said he knew nothing about it. He only mentioned nearly 3 years after this that he saw them with the bomb suitcase when the CIA threatened to cut off all funding. Also he said that Fhimah had shown him 6 kilos' of explosives[20] lying in a drawer in an open plan office that was shared with other companies.

So what might explain Tony Gauci changing his mind over and over? I believe he started as an honest man[21] who wanted to help solve an awful terrorist attack. When the reward money is made public his brother Paul realizes that there is a chance to get $millions in reward. Paul pressures his brother to "remember" so Tony keeps going to the police with new details and new sightings. The only problem is that he keeps seeing someone who is 6ft, over 50 years old, heavy build and dark skinned- nothing like Megrahi. And yet many of these sightings coincide (just about) with times that Megrahi was in Malta. My suspicion is that someone is feeding Paul with info, he in turn is pressuring his brother, who of course gets most of it *wrong*.

---

[17] Giaka claimed that Gadaffi and President de Marco of Malta were Masons. When asked in cross examination how he knew this of Gadaffi he said someone told him, when pressed he refused to name him for *security reasons*, when asked about knowing de Marco was also a Mason this fraudster claimed to have forgotten.

[18] Bollier's 1st effort to become an important witness for Lockerbie was a few days after the bombing when he hand delivered a fake letter to the US Embassy in Vienna. He pretended to be a Libyan radio operator in Tripoli with evidence that Gadaffi had planned and ordered the bombing. It had so many obvious lies that the CIA immediately thought it a joke. Since then he has blamed and exonerated Libya depending on which side he hoped was most likely to pay him.

[19] In fact the SCCRC says they were paid "in *excess* of $2M, and $1M" respectively.

[20] Actually he claimed it was TNT, not much use to the case.

[21] Gauci lived a simple life. His passion was his racing pigeons.

Here is one example. Gauci suddenly recalls the man maybe being in his shop in Summer of '87 probably June because he moved shops in April and it was quite some time *after* that date. The man asked for some blankets to be delivered to the Holiday Inn nearby, to room 113. This is all very specific and it happens that Megrahi was at the Holiday Inn, in 1987. The problem is that he stayed at a *different* room [140] on the 3rd April, BEFORE Gauci moved shops, and the description is still of the mysterious taller, darker, older, stockier stranger. Coincidence?

Again, Megrahi was in Malta in September 21st-24th, 1989. Gauci goes to police to say he came in yesterday 25th. Next day he says actually it was last week (when Megrahi *was* there). When asked why he got confused about something happening the day before, instead of the week before, he can't say except that he was arguing with his family and is confused.

Tony says he was "startled because it was him or his twin" yet within a month he is only 50% sure it was the same man. "It must have been 'his twin' because if the man died on the plane it cannot be him." It becomes a farce when he goes on to say that the reason he noticed the man was that his behaviour was exactly like the purchaser in 1988: he went directly to the part of the shop without looking at the front displays, he chose dresses for a child, he asked for a discount, he was suspicious. Now are we to believe that the man's *twin* behaved exactly the same as him? That would be quite impressive.

the SCCRC uncovers the truth.

The SCCRC did a remarkable job in reviewing the mountain of evidence. While they failed in a few important areas, they went the extra mile many more times. For example when they asked to interview Tony Gauci he refused. You can't blame him really, for 12 years he was the key to the prosecution case and had already banked his $2Mil. Would you agree to be interviewed 3 years after being paid? He just wanted to get on with his simple life looking after his pigeons in their shiny new solid gold, diamond encrusted pigeon coop.[22]

The SCCRC could have said "look, we tried, the guy won't talk to us." But no they pressured the UK government to speak to the Maltese government to find a way to compel Gauci to be interviewed. It took 2 years and a special treaty between Malta and the UK just to make Tony talk. Kudos to them. If I was accused of a terrible crime I would definitely want these guys as *my* lawyers.

Another example. One of the "facts" that the judges claimed was not in dispute was that Gauci had identified the mystery buyer as being Libyan. "The man was talking Libyan to me, He was from Libya." It had been noted that the Maltese often referred to all Arabs on the island as 'Libyano', and also that they could tell if someone was from Libya just from talking to them. There were no scientific studies to determine if this was the case or not. So the SCCRC *even* commissioned one, led by Prof. Tim Valentine who gathered a group of Maltese men, approximately Gauci's age, and a group of men both Libyan and other Arab nationalities to see if they could indeed tell the difference. The results showed that about 40% of the time they got it right: which is indeed pretty good going. But it still means they got it wrong a lot more times too. Ah, but Gauci was certain about being able to tell a Libyan from an Egyptian or Tunisian. The problem with this is that the study found that while those who were very confident did get it right more often, they also were the most likely to make mistakes too (42%).[23] As with witnesses who are *sure* that they picked out the correct suspect, confident does not mean *accurate*.

In other words statistically it is likely Gauci got *even this* basic fact wrong.

So whatever faults are in the SCCRC Report, lack of effort was not one of them.

One error they did make was in concluding there was no political interference in the trial.

---

[22] Ok that last bit I made up.

[23] "Decisions described as 'very confident' were more likely to incorrectly classify a non-Libyan as 'Libyan' than decisions made with any other level of confidence. These data suggest that the confidence that the witness expresses should not be used to infer the accuracy of his judgement" "r*esults do not inspire confidence in the trial court's conclusion that this aspect of Mr Gauci's evidence was 'entirely reliable'.*"

Think about the "star witness" Abdul Majid Giaka. The US Grand Jury that indicted Megrahi and Fhimah did so largely on his testimony. The CIA knew right away that he was a liar, a fantasist, and desperate to get 2 things: out of military service and the JSO and to get the $4 Million reward money. He duped the CIA into paying for sham surgery to his arm and back so that he would fail a medical for active duty. He wanted money[24] to start his own car rental business, another occasion he wanted $2000 to buy bananas on Malta and sell them for a profit in Libya. He would promise them juicy intel to string them along as they were desperate for a man inside the JSO. And they got played. As soon as he got the surgery he told them he didn't want to go work at the JSO anymore.

This car mechanic, seconded to Libyan Airlines in Malta, would never be the mole they wanted- Just a rat. And a thieving, shirking rat at that. Having coughed up tens of thousands of dollars they had nothing and decided to cut him loose. He was given an ultimatum. Come up with useful intel or we stop your money.

Giaka suddenly remembers (after 3 years) he saw Megrahi and Fhimah at Luqa Airport the morning of the bombing, with the explosives in a brown Samsonite suitcase. They get him onto a ship in the Med' to be interviewed by US agents and he and his wife are moved to the USA and put in a witness protection scheme.

In cases like this where a defector claims to have explosive intel he would be asked to take a lie detector[25] test. *With Giaka they didn't dare*. Besides they were no longer wanting a double agent to help spy on Libya. Now they just needed a guy to sit in a witness box and lie.

This is who the CIA foisted on the Lockerbie trial. Worse still they tried to hide all the damning intel cables -not only from the defence but from the court and even from the Crown prosecution- Cables that discussed his motives and character. It took months for the defence to get un-redacted access and when they did it was obvious that the CIA knew[26] very well that their star was a fraud. The judges dismissed his testimony and called him a liar.

The problem is that thanks to this CIA jiggery-pokery the Lord Advocate Colin Boyd QC misled the court. The Crown examined the un-redacted cables and Boyd assured the judges and the defence that there was nothing hidden that had any bearing on *either* the bombing or the *credibility* of the witness. His depute Mr Turnbull had examined these redactions and yet stated that these redactions were not relevant to the defence. The Crown fought for months to stop the defence getting a sight of the complete, embarrassing, un-redacted cables. Every

---

[24] Initially they gave him $1000 a month, then $1500 a month, plus surgery costs, and numerous expenses. He once got $2000 for plane tickets for him and his wife, even though as a LAA employee their tickets were free.

[25] Polygraph.

[26] Even after they gave up and granted the defence access to the unedited cables, and having said that was all of them, it turned out there were another 36 cables the Agency had failed to disclose. Had this not been the biggest terrorist trial in UK history, I think the Judges would have stopped the trial due to outside interference and evidence tampering.

defence motion to get access was opposed by Boyd.

Unless there is some innocent explanation for these actions we have to conclude that the CIA conspired to deny the accused critical information that the Crown was duty bound to disclose. Information *damaging* to the prosecution. They should have been charged for a serious crime: conspiracy to pervert the course of justice. We must know if the Lord Advocate and his Deputes were unwitting accomplices or just witless.[27] Anyone could see that the CIA's star witness was lying.

If this does not count as political interference then nothing does. But regardless of the Megrahi case, their actions contradicted every principle of Scottish justice. If the Lord Advocate can stand in front of a judge and mislead him, if he can withhold crucial documents, then justice goes out the window.

---

[27] All 3 are now senior Judges themselves.

did Gauci really say he saw Megrahi?

Contrary to popular belief Tony Gauci never identified Al Megrahi as the mystery buyer who bought the clothes later found in the bomb case.

The most he said was that he resembled the man he had seen more than 2 years previously. The police showed countless photos of suspects on at least 7 occasions. When Abu Talb was identified in the *Sunday Times* as the likely bomber, Gauci told the police that he thought Talb resembled that man, and yet he couldn't pick him out of the mug shots.

Once Megrahi's name was given to the Scottish investigators they arranged another visit to Tony Gauci to see if he could pick out his picture. In doing so they broke numerous police guidelines designed to safeguard against false identifications. This identification was based on a selection of 12 photos, over 2 years after the buyer had been in his shop.

1st the extreme length of time from the alleged encounter to the first time they showed him photos- 9 months. Studies have shown that after such a long time trying to ID a stranger, from an unmemorable and brief encounter, is very likely to result in a misidentification. The final ID was *over 2 years later*.

2nd Police who know the accused's identity should not be present in case they give clues, accidentally or not, that will cause a false ID. There were police and agents from Scotland, Malta and the US all expecting a result that day.

3rd when shown the 12 photos Gauci told them that none of them could be the person he saw because they were all too young by about 20yrs. This was what is called a "non-identifying response" and that should have been the end of it. But instead, breaking police rules:

4th Gauci was asked to look *again* and imagine if he was 10 or 15[28] years older. What on earth does THAT even mean? Imagine him a bit balder? Missing teeth? Wrinkles? Dark circles under his eyes? Gauci (or anyone) was not *qualified* to try such a ridiculous and impossible exercise. Worse still, the police had never done this with Gauci at previous photo spreads. This was a very strong clue that the accused's picture was one of the 12 and put pressure on him to pick one.

5th with this in mind it is not difficult to understand why Gauci chose No 8. remember that he said the man had a full head of hair. His artist's sketch showed a man with an afro hairstyle. This eliminates photos 1, 4, 9, 11 and 12.

He was supposed to be about 50 years of age. This eliminates 3, 5, 6, and 10. who all look

---

[28] The Scottish officer claims he said "allow for any age difference". Detective Scicluna says it was "allow for 10 or 15 years older".

about 20 years old.

On racial grounds we can ignore number 2.

That just leaves photos 7 and 8.

of those 2 remaining pictures, number 8 (Megrahi), is smaller[29] and very poor quality. It has white lines and spots and a strange white scratch. Why would the police include such a poor quality photo unless they had to? So it is almost certain that he will choose Megrahi's photo. As he examines number 8 the police get excited and at least one says to himself "he's going to pick him." maybe he holds his breath, or shuffles his feet or glances to his colleagues. They obviously visually reacted because Gauci becomes upset that he might now become a target.

6th The FBI later provided another photo of Megrahi. The police thought about another photo ID with this more accurate photo but decided against it in case Gauci didn't recognize him! In other words once they thought they had their man they gave up looking.

7th The account of the Maltese officer is very different from his Scots colleagues and adds important details not disclosed to the defence.

The SCCRC criticizes the whole procedure as deeply flawed "..the witness's full response, the...proper context of his selection was ignored, was not recorded and was not disclosed. The reliability of the whole procedure is seriously undermined..." Added to all this is the fact that at this time the Gaucis' are pestering for reward money payments. This partial ID should have been *thrown out*.

The choice of photos is *incredible*. The police are supposed to choose foils who are similar to the description of the suspect. Who Gauci alleged to be 50+, dark skinned, clean shaven, afro style; full head of hair, Arab. The police had 1000's of available passport photos from Maltese immigration.

So why include 4 who look more like teenagers or young students? Why include 5 men who look more European than Arab? With side partings or receding hairlines? Or 1 who appears more like a young African-American and has some facial hair? The only purpose they seem to serve is to be *easy to dismiss as suspects*.

This leaves just 2 possible faces- conveniently side by side, and Gauci has been given a strong hint that the suspect is one of them. Of the 2, Megrahi looks Arab, the other maybe so. Megrahi's photo is by far the smallest of the 12, it is grainy, it is blurry, covered in white dots, has 2 clear horizontal white lines across his face and a weird white wedge shaped scratch across his bushy hair. Why include such a dreadful quality photo when the other 11 are clear, crisp images? It's as if it was the only one available and had to be included because he was

---

[29] Other 11 photos were at least 10-10.3cm width x 10-12.1cm in height. Megrahi's was 8.7cm x 9.6cm

the suspect. With all these clues it would have been a shock if Gauci had NOT picked him out. All this could not have been an accident. The photo spread seems to be a 'fit-up', calculated to secure the ID that the attending police officers were so excited to get. That Gauci said he merely looked like the man he had served didn't matter. that was enough to stop searching.

An even bigger farce was the identification lineup at Camp Zeist. *8 years later*. Out of 12,000 candidates from an agency, the Crown couldn't find a dozen who even *slightly resembled* Megrahi[30]. And NONE were Libyan. According to Gauci the person would now be in his *60s* yet 8 of the 11 were so young they would have been in their *20s* (and one of those would have been *15 years old*!) at the time of Lockerbie. Of the other 3, one was Dutch! The only man who was close in age was a good 4 inches (5'4") shorter than the accused and going bald and he had a moustache! Once again we have to suspect that the ridiculous mismatch here was deliberate.

Sgt. Mario Busuttil who accompanied Megrahi to Holland stated that none of the others in the lineup resembled him *even slightly*. Even worse, unknown to the judges or the defence, Tony had had a magazine article,[31] with Megrahi's photo (identified as the bomber), at home for *at least* 4 months right up until 4 days before the ID parade. Busuttil put it brilliantly when he remarked "that Megrahi's photo had been in the public domain so often that even *he* could pick him out of the line-up although he had never met him."

By time of trial Megrahi (47) had changed so much from the passport photo that Gauci had picked that he looked *nothing like* the younger self who supposedly had walked into Gauci's shop 12 years previously. Also the man should have been in his 60s by now.

But if the ID parade lineup was a farce the dock ID was a joke. Gauci was walked through his statement, then he was actually *shown the photo* of Megrahi which says he is the bomber! and then asked if he could point him out. Incredibly, from a choice of the 2 accused, Gauci was able to point him out as *resembling* the one who sat nearest to him, "Not the dark one."[32] What a joke that this was allowed.

Gauci was 44 in December 1988, Megrahi was 36. The stranger in the shop was 50 years old or older. How could Gauci mistake a man 8 years younger than himself for a man at least 6 years older? How could he think a man who was 5 foot 8 inches be a man who was 6 feet tall or more. Dark skinned vs light skinned, heavy build vs slim. This was not justice.

---

[30] Seriously. Footage of the parade can be seen in the Al Jazeera film *Lockerbie: case closed*. The other foils are ridiculous. They make a total mockery of Scottish police and Scottish justice. The SCCRC didn't see this video.
[31] *Focus* magazine.
[32] Funny because Gauci had always said the buyer was dark skinned.

paying witnesses is wrong.

There was no more colourful character at the trial than Edwin Bollier, co owner of MEBO in Zurich who had supplied 20 of the infamous MST-13 timers to Libya. From day one after Lockerbie, Bollier tried to implant himself into the investigation for the purpose of making money (which he openly admitted).

A few weeks[33] after the bombing he hand delivered an anonymous letter to the US Embassy in Vienna addressed "CIA to the chief USA." He claimed to be a Libyan radio controller who had learned of a plot between Gadaffi, a Mr Zennnousi and a Mr Shebrill SYRIA. The plot involved a Mr Karlheinz, a German who carried the bomb from Tripoli to Zurich and who coincidentally also had "a Pan Am ticket." Adding *"We've heard that you will pay for classified information."* The entire letter was pure fiction and followed a *Sunday Times* article of January 8th which implicated Libya and Iran.

Bollier then used morse code to try to contact the CIA, who quite rightly dismissed it as nonsense. But 2 years after when his timers were linked to Libya he was questioned by the FBI where he admitted the hoax and offered his services to catch the bad guys.

The FBI had the measure of him early on. Reporting[34] that *"BOLLIER is still interested in the reward...BOLLIER sees three possibilities for BOLLIER to receive money from the US government."* The first would see MEBO supply electrical equipment to the US. The second would have him act as a spy for the US and third *"for BOLLIER to receive part of the reward money"* for info on the Pan Am bombing.

Bollier had for years supplied Western technology to East Germany's Security Service, the Stasi. He was well known to the CIA and West German Intelligence. With the fall of the Berlin wall in 1989 he lost a lucrative source of income and would soon face a $32M lawsuit from Pan Am for selling the timers to Libya.

Desperate for cash he tried to play both sides. While seeking to squeeze the FBI for reward money he was doing the same with Libya. After the visit from the FBI he writes to his old friend (Director of Security of Libya's JSO) Ezzadin Hinshiri, telling them that he spoke to the police about the timers.

"I have been asked to whom such timers had been delivered to, and I could proove [sic] them that in 1985 they have been sold to a Mr Khoury in Beyrut, Lebanon." This not too subtle offer to lie was followed by *"I heard you are now minister of Communications, are there any new projects we could participate?"* Mind you he would later tell the FBI *"perjury in return*

---

[33] 24th January 1989.
[34] This interview with FBI is quoted in John Ashton, *Megrahi, You are My Jury,* Birlinn 2012 p.78.

for payments is out of the question." Of course it is Mr Bollier.

But his offer (threat?) was not in vain he managed in March 1993 to get $120,000 from the Libyans[35] for 'expenses' although failed to secure a loan for $1.8M. This coincided with him telling investigators in October 1993 that he had now been reminded that he had also sold 2 of the same timers to the Stasi. In 1994 this changed to 7 timers[36], then at the trial it was back to 2 again.

When he was given the Libyan bribe he immediately told the Swiss police and offered to hold a press conference to discredit Libya. His estimate of the costs? $300,000!

At trial he was destroyed by cross examination and as his lies were exposed he attempted even more.

Bollier claimed that 3 days before the bombing he had been asked by Badri Hassan[37] to bring a brown leather suitcase to JSO's Ezzadin Hinshiri. Bollier was supposedly in Libya to sell another 40 timers to Hinshiri. Incredibly he claimed that the suitcase held a blue baby suit, men and women's clothes, that were a "gift from Hassan to a friend". Cross examined in court he changed his story about the whole incident. This time *he* had bought the blue baby suit himself as a gift for Mr Ali, who was Hinshiri's driver.

Bollier was trying to link the Libyans to the suitcase of clothes but when cross examined he admitted that he had become 'confused' about the baby suit. Now he claimed that the investigators had sent him a "film" about Lockerbie to explain how the baby suit was in the suitcase. It was the film that mentioned the blue suit and he got confused!

In the lexicon of Lockerbie perjury there is a word for all this: BS, or Bollshit.

Nothing makes that clearer than the tale he spins about Libya running out of timers at the beginning of Dec 1988, just before the bombing. According to Bollier there was not enough time to make another 40 timers for the order. So Bollier buys 40 Olympus timers off the shelf and takes them (and the brown suitcase with the clothes and blue baby suit!) with him to Tripoli. This supposedly was just 3 days before Lockerbie. When he sees Hinshiri the JSO official is not pleased- He wants his MSTs and the Olympus timers are too expensive.

Yet Hinshiri does a quick 180° u-turn and tells Bollier he will keep the timers (that are too expensive) that he just said he doesn't want and tells him to go to Abdelbaset's (Megrahi) office for payment that evening. He waits outside his house for 2 hours while a meeting takes place in the adjoined office. There is just one tiny problem with this tale: Megrahi didn't have

---

[35] As unwise and suspicious as this looks was it really any different than the US was doing? Libya no doubt decided that if the Americans could buy witnesses why shouldn't they.
[36] He claimed to have an invoice for 7 timers but "this might have been a plant when the office was broken into." Planted by who?
[37] Badri Hassan was Al Megrahi's business partner at ABH which rented an office from MEBO.

an office next to his house.

Megrahi wasn't there apparently and he didn't get paid. Next day Hinshiri says he wants the timers but for no given reason he now wants to pay for them later. Bollier refused and waited an hour in which time he is sure that the timers were 'taken somewhere else'. So Hinshiri wants MSTs not Olympus which are too dear. Then he wants them and says Megrahi will pay him. Megrahi, uncharacteristically rude, is a no show at his own home/ imaginary office and next day Hinshiri says he still wants them but now he won't pay for them ...Yet. So the timers he doesn't want/does want, he allows Bollier to take away because he is too stingy to cough up for? Then comes the *coup de grace*. On returning to Zurich he notices that one of the timers had been set for a Wednesday at 19.30.

Pan Am 103 blew up at 19.*03* on Wednesday 21st. Presumably another little detail he got mixed up.

Bollier infers that the timer had been set as a trial run and this is confirmed when in January 1989 he is visited by the same Libyan official he had passed the first batch of 5 timers to in 1985. He knows the man only as "Mustafa" though in later years he swears that it wasn't Mustafa after all. But men from the East German *Stasi*. The mysterious official asks if he had noticed that one of the timers had been tampered with? (To draw attention to his own country Libya's involvement?)

Bollier then claimed that he wiped the timer by disconnecting the battery and then goes to his colleague, Meister and tells him about the timer being set for Wednesday 19.30 but of course there is no evidence now as the screen is blank.

So he gives the whole tale about the Libyans setting the timer presumably as a trial run. Although the JSO official is too stupid to disconnect the battery, leaving an evidential trail. Also the timer is too expensive for an operation blowing up a Jumbo jet. But just to prove that Bollier wasn't trying to finger Libya he says that the timers were lying around his Zurich office and someone could have sneaked in and set the timer to implicate Libyans. Hmmm.

We could analyse this whole fairytale point by point but what would be the *point*. Suffice to say these Olympic timers had a straight 24 hour clock setting and as Libya was 1 hour ahead of London the bomb would have gone off at Wed. SIX thirty (18.30) just as PA103 was leaving the tarmac (damn those stupid Libyans).

Bollier then claimed it was this meeting that prompted him to write his bogus letter to the CIA. The tall dark stranger had threatened him and the letter had to be on a "Spanish typewriter." Later he admitted that he wrote the letter *before* the visit.

Even the judges at Camp Zeist weren't buying this nonsense from Herr Fruitcake.

"We do not accept the evidence of either of these two witnesses about this alleged discovery... the evidence of both witnesses about what they claimed to have seen and the circumstances in which they claimed to have made the discovery was so inconsistent that we are wholly unable to accept any of it."

See this is why Scots Law *forbids* mixing testimony and reward money. Like Majid Giaka and Tony Gauci, Bollier had a knack of changing his story depending on whom he was trying to milk for money.

Giaka suddenly remembered that he had seen the accused men with the bomb at the airport. **Gauci** suddenly remembered he sold the shirts he had sworn he hadn't sold. Likewise also **Bollier** remembered he had sold the timers to others. When you dangle huge reward money as an incentive rats like Giaka and Bollier come out of the sewer. Even seemingly decent guys like Gauci are not immune to temptation.

Reward money *destroys* credibility and causes miscarriages of justice. Not one of these 3 witnesses should have been anywhere near the witness stand. The fact that they were used at all indicates just how weak the prosecution case was. The judges at the Camp Zeist trial ruled that both Giaka and Bollier had not told the truth under oath. That is shocking. As 2 of the Crown's 3 star witnesses all their testimony should have been struck off and they should have been charged with perjury. A less serious trial might have been stopped after such blatant false testimony. Added to the attempt of the CIA and then the Prosecution to conceal the truth about Giaka, a braver set of judges would or should have said enough is enough.

At trial Bollier (having implicated Megrahi and Libya) then tried to sink the prosecution's case by claiming that the fragment of timer in evidence was not the same as the one he had been shown before. He tried to say it was one of the timers he had sold to the East Germans. He claimed it had been tampered with but all he did was undermine the defence's position. Harming Megrahi. The big pay day he had hoped for never came and since then he has kept throwing out conspiracy theory after conspiracy theory, even claiming he was offered millions by the FBI's lead investigator Richard Marquise to say it was Libya who were responsible. Even the conspiracy nuts think he is a joke.[38]

---

[38] By the time of the trial he had given up on the FBI millions and was hoping Libya would reward him for helping the defence. If you want a laugh go to his website where there is a weird email to 'former' FBI Agent Marquise warning he has a letter from him offering millions to blame Libya and a photo [not shown] Marquise had sent him showing huge bundles of dollars in 2 open suitcases. Another email asks why Marquise's email server is returning all Bollier's emails undelivered! I kid you not.

the A-Z of the facts of the case.

If we are to solve the crime we must do what the police did not do. Start with *known* facts, see if they fit with all the other facts, decide if any facts might contradict what is known for certain. Despite doing much that was good, Dumfries & Galloway Police too often allowed themselves to be diverted from the task at hand.

So let's start at the very first fact. Then build on this and see if there is a narrative that can explain ALL of the facts.

a) A bomb blew up PAN AM 103 at *19:03* hours on the 21st Dec. 1988, over Lockerbie, Scotland.

b) This was 38 minutes after it left Heathrow airport on time.[39]

c) So here's the first question: why did it blow up so early into an 8hr flight? Any terrorist using a countdown timer would have set the bomb to explode at least 3-4 hours into the flight. Had weather caused a slight delay or the plane had missed its take-off slot a timer would have blown up while the plane was on the tarmac at Heathrow. So the logical deduction is that there was no choice because of the type of device used.

d) And it just so happens that the device used by the original suspects the PFLP-GC was a *barometric* timer that would trigger following a drop in air pressure. As the plane took off the drop in air pressure would trigger the timer after about 7-10 minutes as the plane climbed. The timers used by this group would then count down from 30 or 45 minutes depending on which model was used. Marwan Khreesat had used 30 minute timers in other bombs he created. Thus a Khreesat made device[40] would always explode between 37 and 40 minutes. PA-103 blew up 38 minutes from when its wheels left the tarmac. Had the plane been delayed an hour, a day, or a month it would still only have blown up 38 minutes after takeoff. That was the 'beauty' of his beastly design.

e) His cell was arrested in Germany, 2 months before Lockerbie, & then all but 2 were released for *lack of evidence!* (Khreesat as a double agent was whisked back to Jordan with a phone call). Bombs in radios, Pan Am timetables, explosives, timers, etc. were somehow not

---

[39] The myth that *Maid of the Seas* was running late otherwise the plane would have been over the ocean is just that: a myth. It was 4 minutes late because a passenger was still in an airport bar with friends when the call for final boarding went out. He ran for the gate but was too late, lucky is not the word. No plane gets in the air right away. It has to taxi to the runway, get clearance etc. then take off. Pan Am 103 was on schedule as it left Heathrow.

[40] Those who claim the PFLP-GC were not responsible never get tired of saying that Marwan Khreesat denied he had built devices within a *twin-speaker* model of Toshiba 'Bombeat' radio cassette player. *Well he would wouldn't he?* Would you admit to building the bomb that killed 270 (mostly American) people and you are in custody. But he did say that he saw such a device in Hafez Dalkamoni's car. Also once he *had* told the FBI the 5th device *was a twin speaker* model but since he refused to testify the defence could not question him on this.

enough evidence. There was a missing radio bomb, & active terror cells in Malta, Yugoslavia, Sweden & *LONDON*. The judges were wrong to claim that a PFLP-GC device could not have been used to blow up PAN AM 103.

f) So assuming that the bomb went off as planned we can deduce that the bomb was introduced at *Heathrow*.

g) Did anyone see the primary suitcase at Heathrow? As it happens yes. John Bedford told the police that he had loaded container AVE 4041 on the afternoon of the bombing with 6 cases. He left the container for a tea break and when he returned about 30 minutes later he noticed "a brown or maroon Samsonite hardshell suitcase" flat on the floor of the container. 2 of his colleagues also saw a case there.

h) The position of the case turned out to be exactly where the bomb was known to have been placed. Most significantly his description of the case was given BEFORE investigators knew what the bomb suitcase was for sure. Crucially it was in the container a full hour before the feeder flight from Frankfurt, Pan Am 103a, arrived. So it *could not have come from Malta or Germany*. Bedford was the ONLY person to describe the exact case at any of the airports.

i) The Crown case was that Megrahi and Fhimah conspired to place a bomb on the plane at *Malta*. Since Fhimah was supposed to be the only one with security clearance who could do this it was unfortunate that they could not even show that he was at the airport that day. Fhimah was acquitted and Megrahi became a conspiracy of ONE. The prosecution could not demonstrate how Megrahi got the bomb on the plane at Malta. The prosecution could not even present a plausible method of anybody doing so. Or even ANY method. The judges described this as *"a major difficulty"* for the Crown's argument. That's the understatement of the decade. It is no wonder because the bomb was placed in London.

j) Luqa airport was one of the *most secure in the world*. A few years previously a horrendous hijacking[41] had cost 58 lives. In response the military had a heavy presence guarding *every* part of the airport. To make things harder Luqa used a unique system to prevent anyone smuggling a bomb onto any plane. Check-in staff and baggage loaders were not told which planes they would work on until they arrived on shift. Additionally the flight dispatcher would call the ramp loader to get the number of bags that were put on the plane. He then called the check-in desk to make sure the same number of bags had been checked in at the desk. If the 2 totals did not match then the plane didn't take off until each bag was reconciled with a passenger. If necessary everyone would be told to disembark & collect their bags until security resolved the problem. Flight KM-180 left Luqa Airport on the 21st Dec with 55 bags. The correct number. Compared to security at Frankfurt it was airtight. Never mind the shambles at Heathrow. If you wanted to place a bomb on a plane you would not choose

---

[41] The US tried to blame even this on Gadaffi.

Malta.[42]

k) How might the bomb get airside through Heathrow security? Well it happens that security chief Ray Manly had reported[43] a security breach near to Pan Am's loading shed in the early hours of that morning. The airside door padlock was cut. Heathrow Airports Ltd also found that 779 security passes had either been lost or stolen in the previous 6 months.

l) Crucially the bomb case managed to get into the exact position needed to cause a fatal explosion. It was positioned flat, with the handle facing away so that the bomb was at the *extreme left side* of the suitcase, against the *left hand side* of the container just a few inches from the hull of the plane.

m) Despite this it only made a fairly small 20 inch hole in the plane, de-pressurization caused the plane to tear itself apart. The explosion itself did not do an enormous amount of damage even to suitcases nearby. The clothes surrounding the bomb absorbed most of the blast.

n) The cases next to and behind and above the bomb case were badly damaged but the cases next to these had very little damage. Dr Morag Kerr has demonstrated conclusively that the case John Bedford saw (the "Bedford Case") was the bomb.

o) She estimates that if the bomb had been oriented so that it was on the right of the suitcase the plane's outer skin may not have ruptured and the plane might have been capable of landing safely. The odds of this happening by chance after two other flights are astronomical.

p) Her book[44] is a masterpiece of forensic examination, raising the question, how could the forensic specialists at RARDE have missed this. It doesn't need saying that on her evidence- which no one has even attempted to refute- *Megrahi could not have been involved* as he was 1500 miles away in Tripoli. Alibis do not come better.

q) What are the chances of a bomb magically negotiating the very strict Maltese security measures, escaping X-ray detection in Frankfurt, unloaded randomly at Heathrow and yet being placed within inches of the only spot that would guarantee the plane blew up? None.

r) Has any terrorist *ever* tried to send a bomb on not just one but two feeder flights? Maybe, but it makes the attack 3 times more likely to fail.

s) So the plane blows up exactly to the minute that a Khreesat made PFLP-GC bomb would explode, was seen by 3 baggage handlers in the container (over 1 hour) before the bags from

---

[42] Once a month without warning this was tested to see if a bomb could get through the system.
[43] Not one Scottish police officer interviewed Manly after he reported the break-in. He was not called to testify at either the *Fatal Accident Inquiry* or Megrahi's trial. The defence were not told of this crucial witness.
[44] *Adequately Explained By Stupidity? Lockerbie, Luggage and Lies*, Matador, 2013. She traces every bag going through Frankfurt onto Pan Am 103, Every bag in the container at Heathrow, she proves where each of the blast damage cases were in the container, what damage each suitcase suffered, from what direction they were damaged and how only the Bedford case could be the bomb. It is meticulous and dispels all doubt.

Frankfurt arrived, placed in the only spot certain to cause a crash, on the same day as the padlock[45] on a door to the airside loading shed was deliberately cut. How did the police allow themselves to be sent chasing false clues to first Frankfurt and then to Malta? They were told that *most* of that container's luggage was from Frankfurt. So they assumed the bomb came on that flight.

t) In the run up to Lockerbie there were at least 3 warnings of an imminent bomb threat to a Pan Am jet between Frankfurt & the US in December, that flight went via London. The terrorists were described as a Palestinian group not affiliated with the PLO.[46] If the PFLP-GC were no longer capable of blowing up a plane then where did these 3 warnings come from? Needless to say the victims' families just want to know why these bomb threats were ignored and why some people knew of them while the ordinary public did not. In what must be a classic example of British bureaucratic incompetence we were told that one of the factors that led to the warning (19th Dec.) not being distributed at Heathrow was a shortage of colour photocopies. Now that I *do* believe.

u) One warning was called into the US Embassy at Helsinki. It was dismissed as a hoax, but was still posted at the US Embassy in Moscow, hence so many cancellations by embassy staff to various Pan Am flights from Europe. A 2nd similar warning was given by the DIA.

v) The 3rd is the most disturbing. Special branch arrested a Palestinian radical 6 months before Lockerbie, he turned out to be a Mossad double Agent. He had infiltrated the London cell of a PFLP terror group. In anger Mossad's London Station chief was expelled with 4 other agents- decimating Israel's ability to monitor threats in the UK. Yet in Nov. 1988 Mossad informed MI6 that one of the PFLP groups would sabotage an airliner in the run-up to Christmas. The Thatcher government dismissed it as Mossad trying to get back in MI6's 'good books'.

w) Did complacency or pride allow Lockerbie to happen? That must be investigated.

x) Assuming the PFLP (hired by Iran) did get the bomb to the UK how else might they have slipped it into the unguarded Pan Am luggage container AVE4041?

y) One option is that during extensive refurbishment of Terminal 3 someone slipped in by cutting the padlock that accessed airside as reported by Ray Manly (see above under k). With a stolen security pass, & little security this would not have been difficult.

z) Another needs investigation. Coincidently 1 flight a day arrived at Heathrow from Tehran that afternoon & departed from pier 5 at 16:59pm. This was Iran flight IRA4703. Pier 5 was

---

[45] The excuse given for the break-in was that it was actually a break-out. Night shift broke the padlock (on the other side of the door from them) to avoid taking a longer detour to get home.
[46] PLO, Palestine Liberation Organization. The PFLP-GC opposed the PLO because they were negotiating with Israel.

reportedly 200yds from the Pan Am interline shed where the bomb was placed during Bedford's tea-break. With numerous baggage handlers of all nationalities, someone with overalls pushing a suitcase on a luggage dolly would not have aroused a second glance.

a piece of fibreglass the size of a fingernail changes everything.

Megrahi was convicted mostly because of the evidence from a 1cm² piece of fibreglass from a printed circuit board (PCB). This tiny fragment, the size of a fingernail supposedly linked only Libya[47] to the bomb.

Ironically should Megrahi's appeal ever be heard he will almost certainly be cleared mostly by an even tinier piece of evidence. The 2 small copper tracks at the bottom of the fragment are less than 1mm thick, yet tests carried out on them proved beyond doubt that this fragment could not have come from any of the timers supplied to Libya. What is worse this was known to the police and the forensic experts at RARDE as early as 1991 and they chose to ignore it. It wasn't until 2008 that tests (commissioned by the defence) demonstrated conclusively that the fragment, found in the collar of a blast damaged grey shirt[48] recovered in a field 20 miles from Lockerbie, *was from a **different** circuit board than those supplied to Libya*.

In 1985 the Libyan intelligence service, the JSO, approached the Swiss manufacturing company *MEBO* owned by the colourful Edwin Bollier. They asked for 20 timers initially with the promise of 1000s more. Most of the parts were available commercially but the crucial part, the motherboard, had to be custom made. Based on the design of MEBO technician Ulrich Lumpert, the PCB was manufactured by another Swiss company named *Thuring AG*, who provided MEBO with 24 circuit boards exactly to their specifications. When the fragment found near Lockerbie was matched to this design the police only had eyes on Libya from then on.

In Spring of 1992 The police took the fragment and a sample of the MST-13 circuit board supplied by Thuring to have metallurgy tests carried out by Dr. Rosemary Wilkinson at Strathclyde University. She examined them both under an electron microscope. While she found that both the fragment and the sample board were made of material typical of most circuit boards there were some issues. 1st of all she noticed that the fragment showed none of the signs usually associated with an explosion (more on this later). 2nd she examined the copper track lines on the fragment and discovered that they were coated with a mask consisting of 100% pure tin. This was unusual because the sample board's coating was an alloy[49] of 70% tin and 30% lead. The process whereby pure tin was applied was by dipping the PCB in a tin solution and this process is only used in "DIY" or "home made" components. It is not what you would expect from a circuit board produced commercially

---

[47] The fragment (known as PT/35[b]) was wrongly matched to the circuit board from an MST-13 timer. Only 20 were made and supplied solely to Libya in 1985.
[48] Evidence item PI/995.
[49] This mask allows components to be soldered onto the PCB. The reason pure tin was not used in the electronics industry was because it required components to be affixed within a few weeks.

such as the board from Thuring AG, that she also analysed.

She informed the police of her findings and speculated that although unlikely, perhaps the lead in the alloy had evaporated during the intense heat of the explosion but *urged* them to run tests to confirm this hypothesis. Neither the police nor the experts at RARDE bothered to do this even although:

"finding only tin instead of tin/lead was without exception regarded by all the experts...as being the most interesting feature, as it was so unusual." (memo from DCI Williamson)

In the Joint Forensic Report of the bombing, finally released in 1991, no mention is made of the different tin coating, in fact Mr Feraday in his report and also in his trial evidence *falsely* claimed that the fragment's [PT/35(b)] *"tracking pattern & materials were similar in all respects"* to the Thuring boards (that made up the timers supplied to Libya).

At trial the head of manufacturing at Thuring, Urs Bonfidelli, confirmed that the tracking mask was made of tin so that seemed to answer the problem. Even the defence team didn't think to question him further. *That was their biggest mistake.* Because unknown to them the term used in the PCB industry "tinning" applied to coatings of tin/lead alloy. No one thought to ask him what compound Thuring made their boards from. When the defence finally questioned him years after the trial his response was devastating. Thuring *ONLY* used a 70/30 tin/lead alloy in all their printed circuit boards. *Never* a coating of *pure* tin. In fact the method of coating PCBs in pure tin involved an entirely different manufacturing process: which they were not equipped for. Here was proof 100% that the fragment found was not "similar in all respects" to those supplied to Libya. Had this one simple question been asked at the trial it is inconceivable that Megrahi could have been found guilty.

As the FBI Agent who led the US side of the investigation, Richard Marquise,[50] observed:

"without PT/35(b), there would have been no indictment."

The case against Megrahi and Libya had been thin to start with. Apart from Megrahi being at the airport in Malta where the bomb *might* possibly have begun its 3 flight journey, and a passing resemblance to the man who bought the clothes from a shaky witness, everything else was inferential at best. The only link to Libya was this fragment and now that link was broken. Unless of course Dr Wilkinson's 'long shot' theory that the explosion caused the lead to evaporate could be verified.

---

[50] As we will see later Richard Marquise and Det Supt. Henderson were aware that the link to Libya provided by this tiny fragment was extremely fortuitous. In fact they speculated that it *might have been planted by the CIA*. This was probably because of the way the Agency was sneaking about, keeping ahead of the Police and FBI investigation. They decided to give them the benefit of the doubt agreeing that the CIA probably wouldn't have done this (although they had done much worse). We can only wonder if now, knowing that the fragment *is* a careful imitation, they would be so charitable.

So Megrahi's appeal team commissioned the tests that *should have been done* by the police in 1991. They hired two separate, independent experts in explosions who had impeccable credentials. The results were a death blow to the case. First of all Dr Jess Cawley[51] noticed that a tiny blob of lead solder on the circuit board's relay pad (the bit that looks like a number 1) was intact. If the explosion could not even melt this small amount of lead solder then there was no way it could have evaporated *all* the lead from the tracking. An element has to melt before it can evaporate. Next he took a PCB with the same tin/lead alloy as the Thuring boards and added a small blob of solder to match PT/35[b] & subjected it to extreme heat in a furnace exceeding that of a Semtex explosion. In an explosion using Semtex the blast causes a momentary flash of very great temperature and then nothing. He measured the length of time taken for the blob of lead solder just to melt at 1000°C degrees: 4 seconds. Far hotter and longer than any explosion from the Lockerbie bomb. Certainly not enough to make all the lead completely evaporate altogether and not even leave a trace.

Finally proof beyond any doubt. The fragment of timer did not match the Libyan timers. The final thread of the crown's case had melted & now evaporated unlike the lead on the fragment! But this raises the most serious problem. This fragment was almost identical in every way to the Libyan MST timers (including the cut out corner curve). So if it was a very careful forgery then we have to know:

Who made this fragment to look like the Libyan timers? The tracking & layout matches the Thuring boards, but not the tinning. So was someone trying to frame them? And how did it find its way into evidence if it was not part of the bomb?

---

[51] Metallurgist with 35 years experience, formerly senior lecturer at Sheffield Hallam University.

bad forensics convicted Megrahi, good forensics will clear him.

What about evidence item PF/546 found on Christmas day 1988, just 4 days after the disaster, it was a "piece of yellow wire soldered to the +ve of a Duracell 1.5V battery." Detective Wm. Grant recalled it was AA size. Because the wire was soldered it would appear not to be from a regular appliance but some home made or improvised device or (ID). So the question is: was this improvised device (ID) identified as belonging to an improvised *explosive* device or (IED)? And were the forensic experts at least suspicious that it was?

It was one of the very first pieces of crash site evidence sent to the forensic techs at RARDE for examination at the beginning of January 1989. Yet it seems to have been ignored or discounted. It never appears in any notes or reports and was returned to the warehouse of Lockerbie items a month later (8/2/89). What happened to it after that is anyone's guess but it was probably destroyed along with many other items in 1990. It wasn't the only clue Feraday ignored. Item PB/1356 "lump of charred molten material, Duracell battery and a piece of red wire." was clearly in the explosion.

Another item is PI/588. Feraday examined it and "he could not rule out as part of a barometer." Also missing. No wonder the Judges found no evidence of a barometric bomb, not if all these suspicious items were excluded from evidence.

What is really weird is that the bombs made for the PFLP-GC terror group by Marwan Khreesat consisted of a detonator powered by 4x 1.5V AA size batteries which had wire soldered to one end. This was an astounding clue that was ignored, worse still destroyed before the forensics report had even been written.

Why did the police ignore such a massive clue that might have been part of the bomb? Well in the first weeks of the inquiry they learned that the Pan Am luggage container numbered AVE 4041 was where the bomb had been placed. Since *most* of the luggage in this container was baggage from flight Pan Am 103a from Frankfurt, they guessed that the bomb had been transferred from that flight. *Wrong again.* 6 items in AVE 4041 had come from other flights earlier that afternoon. It was inexcusable to discount the possibility that one of them contained the bomb. Even when they learned that an extra bag[52] was put in the container at Heathrow that shouldn't have been, they only had eyes on Frankfurt.

Dr. Morag Kerr[53] has proven with forensics exactly where the primary case was in the baggage container, that it was in the bottom layer of luggage, that the Toshiba cassette

---

[52] Matching the description of the bomb case.
[53] She is a forensic expert and secretary-depute of the *Justice for Megrahi* pressure group. Her book '*Adequately Explained By Stupidity: Lockerbie, Luggage and Lies'* is unanswered and unanswerable. Her booklet *Lockerbie fact and fiction* is available online and a great overview of the whole case.

recorder was counter-intuitively packed down[54] the left hand side of the case, that the case was placed flat at the left hand side of the floor of the container AVE4041, with the handle facing inwards. Had it been in any other position. Had it been facing the opposite direction. Had it been just a little further away from the inner skin of the plane's hull it would not have caused a fatal explosion due to decompression and Pan Am 103 and her passengers might well have made it safely back to ground.

She has done this simply by examining the available forensic evidence without blinkers. The Lockerbie bomb was not a very big one relatively speaking. It consisted of about 350-450g of Semtex housed inside a Toshiba 'BomBeat' RT-SF16 cassette recorder. It caused massive damage to a few adjacent suitcases and punched a small hole in the fabric of the plane. The suitcases next to those in contact with the bomb case suffered much less damage. By looking at all those damaged cases she has managed to recreate exactly where the bomb was, where each of the six legitimate cases loaded into the container that afternoon were positioned. She has traced every bag loaded on the flight from Malta, every bag transferred at Frankfurt to Heathrow. Her book (though at places hard reading for this lay-person) is a masterpiece of forensics. And the question she asks is if she could do this why could the experts at RARDE not do the same?

No police force wanted the bomb at 'their' airport. The Scottish police pointed the blame at Frankfurt. The German police (BKA) blamed Heathrow- right back at them. Then it seems both were happy to blame Luqa Airport in Malta. Problem? Luqa Airport's security was extremely tight, especially when contrasted with the shambles at Frankfurt and Heathrow.

From one of the suitcases belonging to DIA Agent Charles McKee we can see that the blast damage was mainly to the bottom corner of the upright suitcase. If the bomb was on the 2nd layer of luggage then the damage to McKee's case would be higher up. This proves that the bomb was on the floor of the container. Exactly where John Bedford claimed he saw a dark brown or maroon Samsonite hardshell suitcase, already loaded in container AVE 4041 a full hour before the feeder flight from Frankfurt had even touched down.[55] Luggage from the feeder flight PA103a was then loaded on top of the others. The bomb was placed at Heathrow. Not Frankfurt and *certainly not Malta*. What is important to keep in mind is that John Bedford is the only person to see the bomb suitcase on the day of the bombing. Crucially Bedford described the exact case in the exact position of the bomb months BEFORE forensics had established that a brown Samsonite case housed the bomb. Before they knew where it had been placed. He could *not* have been influenced by media reports like so many of the Crown's so called 'witnesses'. He had loaded six cases that afternoon in the Pan Am interline shed. He went for a tea break and about 30 minutes later when he returned

---

[54] This alone proves the case was placed by hand in the container by the bomber. If he was leaving it to chance he would have put the bomb in the **middle** of the suitcase to 'hedge his bets.'
[55] Of course Megrahi was 1500 miles away in Libya.

he noticed that the floor of the container was covered by the upright cases along the back, and 2 cases lying flat across the front. AVE4041 had been left unattended during this time.

As with previous miscarriages of justice as a result of sloppy forensics by RARDE experts Hayes and Feraday, the data was there all *along*. The evidence was badly interpreted, the conclusions too dogmatic, and evidence that contradicted their theory ignored and in some cases suppressed. Sadly, it seems, they saw it as their duty not to follow the evidence wherever it might lead but to assist the police to get a conviction. Hayes and Feraday got their report wrong on a massive scale and as a result sent the police in completely the wrong direction. And yet again they sent yet another innocent person to jail for a long time.[56]

Had the police acted on the witness statements of 3 baggage handlers at Heathrow that afternoon, and on Ray Manly's evidence of a break in at Heathrow, near the Pan Am interline shed, early that morning they would have flooded the airport with cops, collected fingerprint evidence, quizzed anyone seen that day in the vicinity, studied cameras and whatever else they should have done. Bedford claimed his colleague S. Kamboj had admitted to loading the brown case into the container, whereas Kamboj denied this[57] to the police. Just this one fact alone ought to have resulted in 'alarm bells sounding' and them poring all over his story and his private life. They didn't. Like Ray Manly's statement of a break-in that was not even followed up! This was a disgrace. So early on in the investigation the police should (as Morag Kerr says) have "cast a wide net".

The police were far too keen to move the scene of crime to first Frankfurt and then Malta: at any cost. Maybe pressure was applied from above, who knows? Heathrow had been recently privatized by Margaret Thatcher and BAA, owned by Heathrow Airport Ltd., would not have wanted to take the blame for the awful state of security there.[58] Nor would they relish the inevitable lawsuits for negligence. 3 very specific bomb threats had been received. Neither the Thatcher[59] government, nor the company whose duty it was to protect air passengers, had revealed the danger to the public. And probably as a result 270 people died[60].

---

[56] Hayes was criticized for the wrongful conviction of Judith Ward [17 yrs in jail], 7 of the Maguire family [16yrs each] Feraday faulted for Danny MacNamee (11yrs), John Berry (8 yrs), Hassan Assali (20 yrs). Megrahi? (10 yrs). Lives ruined.
[57] I am in no way implying that Kamboj was anything other than a decent, hard working, 100% innocent, baggage handler. But the contradiction should have alarmed the investigators.
[58] In the 6 months prior to Lockerbie at least 779 security passes were reported lost or stolen.
[59] See below for numerous possible reasons Thatcher had to skew the investigation away from Heathrow.
[60] They did tighten security measures- a week after Lockerbie!

if in doubt blame Gadaffi.

The CIA were obsessed with Gadaffi, a whole group were actively trying to destabilise his government. And seeking another pretext to bomb Libya again (as they had in 1986).

As world renowned linguist and social critic, Noam Chomsky observed:

"By the early 1980s, it was clear that Communism wasn't going to remain usable as a threat for much longer, so when the Reagan administration came in, they immediately focused on "international terrorism." Right from the start, they used Libya as a punching bag.

Then every time they had to rally support for aid to the Contras [61] or something, they'd engineer a confrontation with Libya. It got so ludicrous that, at one point, the White House was surrounded with tanks to protect poor President Reagan from Libyan hit squads. It became an international joke." [62]

The CIA was aware of MEBO and its dealings with Libya by 1985, and by March 1988 the CIA had connected MEBO to 3 timers seized in Togo and Senegal. It is certainly possible that given their mission to destabilize and overthrow Gadaffi, they could have had a fragment like an MST-13 timer ready to be pulled 'off the shelf' and waiting for a major terror attack to happen. They would have seen Lockerbie as the perfect opportunity to implicate Libya. The fragment of timer was made to look like the ones sold only to Libya. But it was NOT the same: Amateurish 'tinning' and with a pure tin coating. No explosive residue, produced some time 'later' than the sample[63] produced by Thuring AG. The police *and* Dr. Hayes and Mr Feraday at RARDE knew fine that they differed.

"there is nothing quite so lethal as a policeman, or a prosecutor, or indeed a forensic scientist, who is absolutely and sincerely convinced of a suspect's guilt." Dr. Morag Kerr.[64]

Without this counterfeit fragment (PT/35[b]) the investigation would have stayed focussed on the PFLP-GC terror group. Without this fragment the facts point to Heathrow and a PFLP-GC 'barometric' bomb on behalf of Iran. The timer fragment was a massive 'red herring' that destroyed the investigation. It would not be the first time the CIA had fabricated evidence and likely not the first time it had done so to blame Libya[65]. The Agency withheld its link to

---

[61] Nicaraguan terrorists, drug dealing, thugs who butchered mid-wives, teachers and peasant farmers.
[62] Noam Chomsky, *How the World Works*, Penguin 2012.
[63] Expert Michael Whitehead also stated the copper foil for the Thuring board "was manufactured some time earlier than the copper foil for PT/35[b] or *rather PT/35[b] was manufactured later*". PT/35[b] and DP/347[a] "came from two similar but *clearly different* copper clad laminates".
[64] *Adequately Explained By Stupidity*, p 187-188.
[65] There is strong suspicion that the CIA had planted working MST-13 timers to implicate unwitting Libyans in both the Senegal and Togo 'sting' incidents. Charges were dropped through lack of evidence. Add Lockerbie & it is strange that all 3 incidents involved these precise timers that were sold to Libya.

MEBO from both the FBI and the Scottish police. They delayed and tried to block the Scots' police visit to MEBO and got there first. They persuaded disgraced[66] FBI expert Tom Thurman to lie to the Scottish police and the US Grand Jury that indicted Megrahi, Fhimah and of course Libya.

Thurman took a couple of days to ID the timer, "since he knew about MEBO before Lockerbie". Yet he claims that he spent literally months searching through FBI files to solve the mystery.

He hid this from his Scots colleagues and bizarrely says that "we knew what (MEBO) was really, but didn't want to go there directly, we wanted to make sure we'd ruled out other possibilities." He didn't tell the Scots until late September yet FBI visited MEBO in August.

The CIA further delayed the Police until late November and tried unsuccessfully to block their visit, and when that failed they sent their own agents there in the days before the Scottish police could interview Edwin Bollier. We must ask why?

---

[66] Thurman was found to have altered reports in 30 out of 52 FBI cases reviewed: often to favour the prosecution. Having given false evidence, he was prohibited from giving expert testimony. Similarly in overturning John Berry's conviction the Judge declared *"Mr. Feraday should not be allowed to present himself as an expert in electronics."* this was in 1993, - 7 years before the Lockerbie trial!

suspicious evidence.

When considering the numerous evidence items that seemed to have been tampered with, the SCCRC tended to give the benefit of the doubt to the forensics experts, police, the Crown prosecution, the CIA and FBI and Britain's MI5, for many discrepancies that could not be explained. Had they known that the central piece of evidence was a clever copy would they have altered their view? The evidence for a Heathrow bomb with a barometric timer was extensive. But all that was rejected because of this fragment of MST-13 timer. Malta became a possible airport for the bomb because of this timer. Pointing to Libya. Without it the case against Libya collapses. And the evidence of a barometric bomb placed at Heathrow suddenly all makes sense again.

One of the most suspicious episodes involves the crucial evidence bag PI/995 which was a fragment of charred shirt collar that housed not one but 4 items linking Libya to the bombing. Fragments of radio from an RT-SF16 Toshiba radio, a fragment of a users manual for same model, little bits of mesh from the speaker, and charred fragment of timer (PT/35[b]). you know what they say once is chance, twice a coincidence but 3 and never mind 4 times? and nothing else. How likely could 4 differing bits of fragments from the bomb, the radio, the manual, all get embedded in the collar?

If that is being paranoid then why was the evidence label altered surreptitiously?

Why change an evidence label from "CLOTH CHARRED" to "DEBRIS CHARRED", and do so in such a subtle way as to escape detection until it was forensically examined and defence QC Richard Keen managed to spot it? Each letter had been very carefully changed i.e. '**D**' covers up C, '**E**' made out of the L, '**B**' out of O, '**R**' from T and '**I S**' from H. The signature was written by D C Gilchrist who first found the shirt collar on January 13th 1989. Along, with DC McColm. The rules regarding label changes were simple. In the event of an error, score out the original word neatly and initial any change. The implication is that it was not Gilchrist but some other nefarious hand. As if worried that a bag of singed "cloth" might be ignored by the forensics expert at RARDE. Whereas "Debris" invites closer inspection. Now it could not have been that Gilchrist didn't see it was a shirt. He wrote cloth after all. But no one could tell in January that there was debris inside the collar when found. The fragments were not extracted until May 12th at the very earliest.[67] It is hard to avoid the conclusion that the very deliberate alteration to the label had a sinister motive. How hard would it be for a member of US or UK intelligence to tamper with one evidence item either in the MOD run facility RARDE or back at Lockerbie's Dexstar storage warehouse? Probably the latter would be easiest. It is then a matter of waiting to be found. When 18 months pass without progress

---

[67] See below for further anomalies with this evidence.

this is taking too long to link with Libya the CIA points Thurman in the direction of MEBO, and then (we know) asked him to lie about it to both the Scottish investigation and the Grand Jury. This fragment altered the entire investigation. It sounded crazy, to those unfamiliar with the CIA and MI5 history, until the fragment that made the whole case against Libya was found to be nothing of the kind.

There are only 4 ways for PT/35[b] to get into the shirt collar.

a) it was part of the bomb that somehow managed to survive the blast. If so why did the plane explode at only 38 minutes: consistent with a barometric trigger, in a bomb placed exactly the right place, despite supposedly two previous feeder flights. Unlikely.

b] it was placed in the bomb or the case by the PFLP-GC to implicate Libya and not the Palestinians. This is very unlikely as there would be low odds of it surviving let alone being found and identified as Libyan.

c] it was placed in the collar, on the hills left to be discovered. Unlikely as it could have been missed, or fell out of the shirt and lost.

d] it was inserted in evidence after the shirt was found, bagged and then the label was changed. None of the options a, b, c, above account for the label change.

Needless to say it is not the only evidence with a big question mark hanging over it. I've mentioned the battery with soldered wire that resembled Marwan Khreesat's barometric bombs. Inexplicably ignored and missing. Then there is an item that Mr Feraday could not rule out as from a barometric device. Missing. He never describes it in his notes, takes a picture or a drawing and it has disappeared (probably destroyed in 1990). For Megrahi's 2nd appeal the defence sought many items of fragments, all had vanished: without a record of when.

More suspicious are items found inside the metal identification plate for the luggage container AVE4041 which was folded with fragments of a radio's printed circuit board or PCB, inside it: the fragments AG/145[68] which linked the radio to a model popular in Libya. The only problem with this other key piece of the jigsaw is that the AAIB[69] chief investigator, Peter Claiden (with years of experience) was absolutely certain that there is *no way that the blast caused the metal plate to fold in half* and *no trajectory that bomb fragments would get into this folded metal plate either*. The implication of his testimony is that this too could have been planted.[70] The metal plate was on the outside of the container. So how did the fragments

---

[68] Also weird is that PT/30 (which matched fragments AG/145) was examined and labelled in June 1989 a month after PT/35 but is numbered well out of sequence. The origins of both are very suspicious.
[69] Air Accident Investigation Branch.
[70] It was widely reported that US agents guarded a large item under a tarpaulin for hours until it was removed. It was described as smaller than a car, and searchers were kept away from this by men who were heavily armed. Could that have been the luggage container? If not what? & why the secrecy.

explode out of the container, & then what? Bounce back against the plate just as it gets folded in half? We can see his point. Especially fishy is that these fragments of *paper* substrate- blasted from an IED- are perfectly smooth faced, no blast damage at all, and tested negative for explosive residue. Also they handily had both numbers and letters to easily identify them to a Toshiba RT-SF16.

When accosted about the questionable chain of evidence regarding the timer fragment,

DCI Henderson replied "there are no hidden holes to find because the culprit is in custody - take my word for it!"

Sorry Sir but given what we now know we just can't do that.

At times the Lockerbie investigation resembles a badly conceived 80's board game by Waddingtons.

"CIA get to witness ahead of you- miss a turn"

"Operation Sandwood investigates Crown corruption- Go straight to jail"

"Key piece of evidence turns out to be a fake- GAME OVER!"

the A-Z of PT/35[b].

This 1cm² little fragment was the turning point of the whole investigation and the only evidential link to Libya. Without it the forensic, intelligence data, and witness evidences all point to a Heathrow bomb of the Syrian based Palestinian group, the PFLP-GC, contracted by Iran to avenge their passenger aircraft shot down 5 months before Lockerbie. They had motive, they had opportunity and they had means. Libya had neither, but someone wanted us to think so.

So with so much depending on this tiny bit of timer it is worrying that so many doubts surround its provenance.

a] the evidence label [PI/995] for the shirt collar, containing the fragment of PCB, originally read 'CLOTH (CHARRED.'

b] it was allegedly found by DC Gilchrist 13th January 1989.

c] unusually it was not logged at Dextar until 4 days later on 17th January.

d] at some point between then and 12th May 1989[71] the label is very discreetly altered to read 'DEBRIS (CHARRED)' [72]

e] label ID number PI/995 [actually PI9/95] also looks altered from PT/15 or PT/95.

f] DC Gilchrist accepts responsibility but claims to have no knowledge of doing so and claims he wouldn't have done this. Also says the "D" is not his handwriting.

g] Dr Hayes forensic report notes also raise a number of questions about the provenance of PT/35[b]. RARDE photo 116 and 117 purport to show the shirt before and after dissection. Photo 117 shows all the items found in the collar: labelled PT/35 followed by letters [a] the Toshiba radio fragments, [b] the MST timer fragment, [c] pieces of speaker grill, [d] the toshiba manual fragment. But some fragments in 116 were not at RARDE during May 1989. The SCCRC found that the photo record was wrong, which made the Report wrong. 116 & 117 both show the shirt collar *after* dissection. For a criminal case records *matter*. This is not a minor issue. Doubts about one photo casts doubts on all others.

h] worse, page number 51 of Hayes notes has been alleged to have been inserted at a later date because the following 5 pages had to be renumbered 52-56. Forensic testing for the SCCRC proved that there were no indentations of page 51 on the page underneath, rather writing from some other document.

---
[71] Or maybe even later than this.
[72] Looking at the 'D' in Debris, comparing it with the 'D' in Charred they are obviously different.

i] this problem all stems from RARDE abandoning bound notebooks for loose leaf sheets. And rolls of negatives for ones cut up into strips. This was a serious breach of forensic best practice and may have followed cases where the convictions were overturned on the basis of notebook evidence withheld from the defence. For which RARDE and Hayes were singled out for criticism. Of course with loose pages and negatives there is no way to demonstrate that the evidence is 'kosher' just as there is no way to prove malpractice. But it sure looks suspicious.

j] having discovered the timer fragment he is so excited he calls in his colleague and they agree it could be part of the IED but then for some inexplicable reason they then ignore it for 4 months until Feraday tells DI Williamson. It is then a further 3 months before the police get to see the fragment that could be so crucial.

k] when their joint report is finished Feraday claims that the fragment materials and tracking patterns are the same in all respects as the MST-13 timers sold only to Libya. He was however well aware that there were crucial differences in the make up of the fragment from those used in the MST-13 timers sold to Libya. The tracking was pure tin on the fragment whereas the MEBO boards were a tin/lead alloy [see above]. The copper laminates were also different. He repeated these falsehoods in evidence at trial too.

l] Hayes claimed in court that the fragment of timer PT/35[b] and the fragment of radio PT/30 were not tested for explosive residue. This too was false. Tests had been carried out and proved negative. The test results were not disclosed to the defence.

m] as we know AAIB investigator Peter Claiden all but said that AG/145 was planted.

n] there were only 20 timers made for Libya and yet between the Scots and the CIA they appeared to have 4 of these, or 20%. This is quite a feat.

o] the FBI agent who identified the fragment lied about who supplied this info saying it was the BATF or Bureau of Alcohol, Tobacco and Firearms. When in fact it was the CIA.

p] Thurman also lied about this to the Grand Jury that indicted Megrahi and Fhimah for the bombing. He admitted later *"it was the 1st time he'd 'fronted' for the CIA."* Were there others?

q] he did so at the request of the CIA agent who helped him, "John Orkin" for what reason we do not know, but it was to conceal any CIA involvement in the discovery of the timer fragment. The CIA also repeatedly delayed the Scottish Police so that the CIA could be the first who visited witnesses overseas. Whoever conspired to blame Libya and Megrahi, we may never know, but the fingerprint of the CIA is everywhere on this case.

r] Thurman knew about MEBO timers before Lockerbie but hid this information from the Scottish Police.

s] he claimed it was many months of diligent searching when it was actually 2-4 days.

t] Thurman was found to have testified in areas he was not qualified, altered reports and is banned from court expert testimony. He is no longer with the FBI.

u] getting back to the evidence found in the shirt it is a remarkable coincidence that parts of [1] the radio casing identified as Toshiba RT-SF16 'Bombeat'. [2] Fragments of a manual that could be identified as the same model the RT-SF16. and [3] little pieces of the same speaker and [4] a small fragment of the bomb's timer, could all survive inches from a 1000 degree explosion and still all end up in the same shirt collar. But no bits of timer were found in any other clothing or suitcases from the crash.

v] the piece of timer 1cm^2 happened to be from perhaps the only identifiable part of the timer. The bit that resembles a large numeral '1' and below this twin copper track lines that match the Libyan timers sold by MEBO exactly *(including imperfections!)* and yet it is not one of the boards that Thuring made for MEBO for the Libyan timers. Because it is now known to be an *almost* perfect copy. Who could have done this?

w] when Dr. King, the defence expert for Megrahi's 2nd appeal tested the Radio fragments: they did not match the casing of the Toshiba RT-SF16 model after all. So Hayes was wrong *yet again*.

x] this is important because the Crown claimed wrongly as it turns out, that [1] The PFLP-GC's bomb maker Marwan Khreesat supposedly only made bombs concealed in the single speaker models of Toshiba 'Bombeat' Cassette Recorders.[73]

y] and [2] the crown had alleged that Libya bought 76% of world sales of this model. Although in the 6 months AFTER Lockerbie this was true, in the crucial 3 years before Lockerbie, Libya had only bought 11%, which is much less incriminatory. This model was sold in Khreesat's country: Jordan, and other Middle East countries.

z] this MST-13 timer was the only evidence linking the bomb to Libya. It also implied that any bomb could travel from Luqa – Frankfurt – Heathrow without exploding, which incriminated Megrahi as he was leaving Luqa Airport, the same time as the feeder flight for Pan AM-103a.

aa] a barometric bomb would explode on the 1st leg of the journey so would have to be placed at Heathrow as so much of the actual evidence does indeed point to.

bb] when a piece of evidence is so crucial to the Crown's case it has to be *above suspicion*. With so many unexplained anomalies it really should not have been allowed in evidence.

---

[73] This was false. Khreesat admitted to FBI that *he had* used the twin speaker model. See SCCRC statement of reasons from their 800 page report which is online at www.megrahiyouaremyjury.net

Now that it is known not to be one of the timers sold to Libya, the entire, flimsy case collapses.

cc] would the 3 Judges have accepted the defence had *it* claimed that a 1cm² fragment could overturn all the evidence but had over 2 dozen question marks regarding its provenance? I think we all know the answer.

dd] if PT/35[b][74] really did survive an explosion of 450g of Semtex placed inside a radio (about 1 inch from the timer) how fortunate that the only part of the timer found included the only distinct markings & with the curved cut out section which so helpfully confirmed that it was identical to a boxed type MEBO timer circuit board. Remember that no other fragment of the circuit board was recovered from ANY of the other fragments of clothing in the bomb case. Just a solitary 1cm², fragment that happens to have *3 distinct markings* of a MEBO timer: The relay pad[75] which looks like a big number "1," the copper tracking of two distinct lines with matching imperfections, and the curved cut-out. The probability of this happening is low. Any other part of the timer would have been almost impossible to match. If the person who made this fragment had just got the correct tin/lead alloy on the tinning of the copper tracks, it would have really matched the Libyan timers. But they didn't so thankfully we can tear up the conviction of Abdelbaset Al Megrahi and declare him an innocent man. It is that simple. Posthumous apologies to him (and Colonel Gadaffi too for that matter) are in order.

1 or maybe 2 doubts about this critical bit of evidence would be a concern but dozens? And then to confirm that there was something fishy we now know for certain, that whatever this fragment was it certainly did not come from Libya. The one country that did *not* need to forge an MST-13 timer was Libya.

There were DIA, NSA, and CIA cables, intercepts, and chatter implicating the Iran / Syria / PFLP-GC and at least 3 specific bomb warnings of a Palestinian terror group targeting Pan Am flights to the USA from Germany & London in the weeks before Lockerbie. This might not have been admissible evidence in court but it still existed. That matters.

But there appears to be no such chatter, warnings, cables, etc. regarding a Libyan attack. If there was we *would* have heard of them. That also matters.

Just to be absolutely clear this book is NOT claiming that the CIA planted the timer fragment to blame Libya. It does raise many questions about their suspicious behaviour before, during & after the investigation: including the trial. It does show they had motive.

Obviously the investigators themselves had their doubts:

"Could the CIA have planted the evidence? I don't know. No one ever came to me and said,

---

[74] There is a great entire blog dedicated to this fragment's history: pt35b.wordpress.com
[75] This is part of the circuit board that can have components soldered onto.

'Now we can go for the Libyans', it was never as straightforward as that. The CIA was extremely subtle." Lord Fraser - The Lord Advocate, at time of the indictments.

"*Swiss Inspector Hans Knaus expressed his concerns... The first was that the CIA had planted the chip [PT/35(b)] in the wreckage found at Lockerbie. [DS Stuart] Henderson and I told him this thought had also crossed our minds. Neither of us believed the CIA or any government official would do such a thing, but we had discussed the possibility.*" Richard Marquise, FBI.

Since it can be demonstrated that the bomb was planted at Heathrow, and was not triggered with a Libyan timer, the onus is on the Crown to explain the many, many inconsistencies of the evidential chain. The failure to provide the defence with countless crucial documents that undermined the prosecution's case. The non-disclosure of a witness to the break-in at Heathrow, and also a witness who undermined Gauci's version of events. The mistakes, omissions & deceptions in the RARDE Report. The behaviour of the Lord Advocate's team regarding the CIA cables, the deception by Police officers over millions of dollars paid to witnesses, the unforgivable delays in granting an appeal to a dying man, in what will be remembered as the biggest scandal in Scottish legal history.

It is now up to the Scottish Government to restore confidence in our judicial system for all Scotland's citizens, albeit for a mess that was made by its predecessors.

Thatcher benefits from not investigating Heathrow Airport.

The investigation was too easily pointed in the direction of Frankfurt. While we can see why they thought this way, and the Scots police genuinely thought they were on the right track is it also possible they were nudged this direction by "State interests"?

Why were the Heathrow clues ignored. The Metropolitan Police failed to follow obvious facts that were staring them in the face. Was it wishful thinking that the bomb had not slipped past Heathrow security? Or did persons unknown, or vested interests make sure that Iran was not blamed, and the finger of blame shifted to Libya.

While there is no proof as yet, there were a number of reasons why Margaret Thatcher[76] would want to make sure that suspicion did not fall in her backyard. With the added bonus that one of hers, and the USA's biggest enemies would be blamed for the biggest atrocity on British soil.

We know that former CIA director (and then US President), George H. W. Bush had led a massive and not so secret intelligence campaign to destabilize and overthrow the dictator of Libya, Colonel Gadaffi, lasting over 10 years.

They blamed him for nearly every terror attack in Europe during the 1980's. Lockerbie was a gift to *those obsessed with getting rid of "Mad Dog" Gadaffi*. Since this is well covered in books and websites I will not go into the whole sordid history.

What is less known is Thatcher's triple obsession with [a] Gadaffi, as a result of his supplying weapons to [b] the IRA, and because of Libyan miners who offered money to [c] those she branded "The Enemy Within": the NUM[77] in their year long strike to save their mining jobs.

In 1984-85 she used the resources of the UK's security state in what was to become a personal vendetta to cripple the NUM, and its ferocious leader, Arthur Scargill. We learned from GCHQ whistle blowers how with the help of MI5, NSA and the CIA they infiltrated the miners, used agent provocateurs, disinformation campaigns, planted money in fake accounts, in a dirty year long war, that blighted and divided mining communities the length and breadth of the country.

In 1990 nearly her last two acts in power were 1st to get crippling sanctions against Iraq[78] that would through starvation & disease kill a million Iraqi children and a similar number of adults. And 2nd start a malicious media campaign to destroy Arthur Scargill, and weaken the

---

[76] May 2019 will be the 40th anniversary of her becoming prime minister. I call this our 'Alba Naqba' or *Scotland's Catastrophe*.
[77] Seumas Milne, *The Enemy Within, The Secret War Against the Miners*, Verso- 1994, revised 2004.
[78] Opposed most vocally by- yes you guessed by now: Gadaffi of course.

mining industry in preparation for privatization. All this dovetailed nicely with framing Gadaffi for the Lockerbie bombing.

Scargill was accused of stealing money that had been gifted to the miners from Libyan workers to pay off his mortgage. The 2 biggest Thatcherite newspaper moguls: Robert Maxwell and Rupert Murdoch [or RM²] printed lie upon lie in a year long media frenzy. All the allegations were eventually proved false in court (with eerily similar echoes of the Lockerbie case), and Thatcher herself would fall while Scargill was vindicated. Robert Maxwell would commit suicide rather than be exposed to be the biggest thief of all, embezzling (ironically) his workers pension funds of £100's of millions.

Scargill was 1st accused of taking £163,000 from Gadaffi and 3 guns for some reason. This grew eventually to $9Million, as Britain's gutter press published 'all the lies fit to print'. The Secretary of the NUM, Roger Windsor, was exposed as an MI5 stooge, (who staged his 1984 photo-op with Gadaffi, and nearly ruined the noble miners' cause. Windsor has given contradictory versions of the story, which was probably planned by MI5 given the amount of detail leaked to the press. He was supposed to address a Libyan miners union, not kiss Gadaffi on tv). Ironically Windsor did use the funds for HIS mortgage.

This media onslaught of 1990-91 dovetailed nicely with the Lockerbie case as Libya all of a sudden was the prime suspect for the bombing. How much the two tales intertwined we may never know, but like most folk I am not a fan of coincidence. Pressure on Gadaffi caused him to sever links with the IRA, the reputation of the miners union was damaged by their Libyan ties, and sanctions were tightened on a country that was beyond the control of Western interests. For Thatcher it was killing 3 birds with one stone, or win, win, win! Bush and the CIA played their part; and given what we do know the CIA did over the Lockerbie evidence it is difficult not to draw adverse conclusions about how far they would go to "get their man."

I said there are often multiple reasons why Thatcher would want to see the investigation focus on Frankfurt rather than Heathrow and so here are a couple more. Truth is the first casualty of (a liability) war.

Heathrow was one of the stars of her privatization policy. Ownership passed to BAA & Heathrow Airport Holdings Ltd. and as we should expect security would be seen as not so much a necessity as a burden. If 270 people had died on their watch the implications would have been a disaster for them- at least where it mattered most- financially.

Dr. Jim Swire demonstrated a few years later that little had changed as he successfully boarded a flight from Heathrow to JFK with a fake bomb, using a block of marzipan to mimic Semtex.

What other reason might encourage the investigation's focus elsewhere? Well 2 groups were booked on Pan Am 103 amongst whom no love was lost. Pik Botha, racist apartheid South African Foreign Minister and his entourage of 22, changed to another flight but deny getting any warning of a bomb threat. His opposite number Bernt Carlsson was less fortunate. In fact his suitcase was loaded by John Bedford and ended up right behind the Samsonite bomb case. It was severely damaged but now forms part of the conclusive proof that the bomb was placed at Heathrow.

Carlsson was the UN representative of Namibia in peace accords with South Africa. But he had sworn very publicly[79] to expose the theft of $10Billion in diamonds from Namibia by De Beers. Weirdly he was from Sweden, where Abu Talb was living. He was a close friend of the PLO leader Yasser Arafat, and closer friend of Issam Sartawi murdered by the Palestinian Abu Nidal group. Who like Talb's PPSF and the PFLP-GC were bitter opponents of Arafat and Sartawi. When Abu Talb was arrested in 1989 for other bombings he was found with a quantity of Maltese clothes, watches with missing parts, a barometer missing the part used for timers, and a calendar which had a mark next to the 21st December 1988. He had visited the PFLP terror cell in Malta in October, & may have been there in November to buy the clothes, he also had 4 burnt passports in other names.

On a more personal note for Thatcher was the illegal mining of Uranium from the Rossing mine, in occupied Namibia. Owned by Rio Tinto Group (RTZ). A former director of Rio was Lord Carrington, who resigned from the board to become Thatcher's Foreign Secretary and

---

[79] Appearing in a World In Action Documentary: *The Case of the Missing Diamonds*, He was highly critical of De Beers, RTZ and the South African Government.

In a comment for Berndt Carlsson's death, in the Lockerbie bombing, an editorial in *The Guardian* of 23 December 1988 stated: "Two days before Christmas, two tides flow strongly. One - the greater tide - is the tide of peace. More nagging, bloody conflicts have been settled in 1988 than in any year since the end of the Second World War. There are forces for good abroad in the world as seldom before. There is also a tide of evil, a force of destruction. By just one of those ironies which afflict the human condition, peace came to Namibia yesterday. Meanwhile, on a Scottish hillside, the body of the Swedish UN Commissioner for Namibia was one amongst hundreds strewn across square miles of debris: a victim - supposition, but strongly based - of a random terrorist bomb which had blown a 747 to bits at 31,000 feet."

In investigating Carlsson's murder, Scottish police detective John Crawford stated in his book (The Lockerbie Incident: A Detective's Tale): *'We even went as far as consulting a very helpful lady librarian in Newcastle who contacted us with information she had on Bernt Carlsson. She provided much of the background on the political moves made by Carlsson on behalf of the United Nations. He had survived a previous attack on an aircraft he had been traveling on in Africa. It is unlikely that he was a target as the political scene in Southern Africa was moving inexorably towards its present state....I discounted the theory as being almost totally beyond the realms of feasibility.'*

Let's pray it had nothing to do with *Palestinian* terrorists despising his support for the PLO. That would be the ultimate irony if for 30 years we had been blaming Iran, then again maybe Talb & co. were thinking of 2 birds with one stone also. This is pure conjecture but merits investigation.

Many have called for a special inquiry by the UN into this angle of the Lockerbie Bombing.
"A United Nations Inquiry can be expected to find a different - and much better - explanation for Bernt Carlsson's murder."
The first signatory is Robert Black QC, Emeritus Professor of Scots Law at Edinburgh University.

was immediately put in charge of overseeing the UK negotiations for Namibian Independence. With the fox in charge of the henhouse this helped RTZ to be able to steal as much of the countries resources as it could possible get away with before and after the hand over of power. Carlsson was investigating Rossing which could have seen them going out of business.

The Rossing scandal was one of the darkest most sickening episode in British history, Labour and Conservative governments alike enabled the illegal exploitation of the Namibian people, with appalling conditions for the Black workers who earned a pittance[80] compared to their white colleagues. Segregated, mistreated, lacking any medical facilities for the constant exposure to radioactive dust, it was a microcosm of Apartheid in action. *The Rossing File*, available online, is a thorough expose of Thatcher's hypocrisy in publicly condemning Apartheid while in practice she did all she could to support its grip on South Africa. While it was a good reason to shift the focus of the investigation from Heathrow, to avoid embarrassing attention, it is not possible to say whether there was any connection between Carlsson & the bombing. Coincidentally Iran had an 11% share in the Rossing mine. However a full inquiry would need to investigate every angle, and not dismiss the possibility that PAN AM 103 was specifically chosen because of certain people on board. Only then can we be sure that the whole truth comes out about Lockerbie & put another conspiracy to bed.

Personally I think Thatcher's biggest incentive was to avoid blame for ignoring the warnings of a bomb. Conspiracists tend to ignore basic human instincts over 'deep state' machinations. As a rule look for CYA before CIA.

---

[80] Black workers earned under £2 a day after deductions for squalid overcrowded dorms, described by a journalist as the worst he'd seen in Namibia. Meanwhile whites were highly paid, had their own town with good housing & regular medical checks.

conclusion.

We owe it to Abdelbaset al Megrahi to clear his name of this awful crime. He was a humble family man, with no extremist views, he loved his academic studies, in Wales, the USA, and Libya. He seems to have been sacrificed by international politics to lift the unjust and illegal sanctions[81] forced upon his country, Libya.

As head of Security for Libya's Airline: the LAA, he had dedicated his life *to the security of airline passengers*. Training others to put the safety of passengers first. To be accused of this terrible act of terrorism was the worst thing that could happen to him.

I am saddened that he only saw my beautiful country from behind the bars of Barlinnie and Greenock Prisons. If found innocent he and his family will be due a huge public apology.

On 9/11 as he sat alone in prison and watched the horrors of that day, he wept for those 3000+ souls who died and their loved ones. He died with the shame of still being known as "the Lockerbie bomber." As cancer ravaged his frail body his dying wish was for his and his families name to be cleared. It is the very least we can do.

There are those who still think he was guilty. I urge you to listen to the facts and not the politicians who always have an agenda, and *who serve the powerful not the people nor the truth*.

Therefore we must call for a full public inquiry with the power to subpoena witnesses under oath and any documents relating to Lockerbie, to establish the facts of the Lockerbie disaster. It is *never* too late to find out the *truth*. The 270 people who were taken too soon deserve this. Their souls cry out for justice.

"how long before you judge the people... and avenge our blood for what they have done to us?" Revelation 6:1

---

[81] As a signatory of the Montreal Agreement, Libya had the right to try the accused in Libya. This was impossible because the US and UK refused to hand over evidence against them. Instead the US bullied the UN to impose crippling sanctions against Libya in clear breach of international law.

further study

Books

John Ashton, *Megrahi You Are My Jury. The Lockerbie Evidence*, Birlinn-2012.

the best one volume look at the whole case.

Dr. Morag Kerr, *Adequately Explained By Stupidity? Lockerbie, Lies & Luggage*, Matador-2013. Focuses on the luggage evidence as well as other forensics issues. Exceptional, witty.

Douglas Boyd, *Lockerbie the Truth*. The History Press-2018. Very detailed on the Iranian response to their plane shooting, revenge plan, the PFLP-GC plotting & arrests. Some errors.

Samuel M. Katz, Israel versus Jibril: The Thirty-Year War Against A Master Terrorist, Paragon House, 1993.

although too early to know what we know now, Katz presents compelling evidence of Jibril's PFLP-GC for destroying Pan Am 103. His excellent sources within Mossad show the Syrian/Iranian involvement, and why the Americans chose to blame Libya & not Syria when the latter was the biggest sponsor of international terrorism for decades. That Jibril knew the German PFLP cell was compromised, and he sacrificed them as a distraction. A gold mine.

Websites.

SCCRC 800 page Report on Megrahi's conviction. Available at megrahiyouaremyjury.net

Robert Black QC's blog about the disaster & the trial. lockerbiecase.blogspot.com

Dr. Jim Swire's website. lockerbietruth.com

Popular blog on all things Lockerbie especially forensics. lockerbiedivide.blogspot.com

Everything you wanted to know about the timer fragment. pt35b.wordpress.com

David Wolchover, Barrister, *Culprits Of Lockerbie,* 2016. davidwolchover.co.uk

David's book available to download as a pdf. covers every single part of the whole controversy, point-by-point.

Lastly a list of all those who were murdered. victimsofpanamflight103.org/victims

studying this case it is *easy* to lose sight of those who died & their loved ones left behind.

Printed in Great Britain
by Amazon